BUYING PROPERTY

NativeSpain.com

BUYING PROPERTY IN MURCIA

Debbie Jenkins

NativeSpain.com

First Published in Great Britain 2008 by www.BookShaker.com

© Copyright Debbie Jenkins

All rights reserved. No part of this publication may be reproduced, stored in or introduced into a retrieval system, or transmitted, in any form, or by any means (electronic, mechanical, photocopying recording or otherwise) without the prior written permission of the publisher.

This book is sold subject to the condition that it shall not, by way of trade or otherwise, be lent, resold, hired out, or otherwise circulated without the publishers prior consent in any form of binding or cover other than that in which it is published and without a similar condition including this condition being imposed on the subsequent purchaser.

Typeset in Trebuchet

DISCLAIMER

While all attempts have been made to verify information provided in this publication, neither the Author nor the Publisher assumes any responsibility for errors, inaccuracies or omissions. Any slights of people or organisations are unintentional.

This publication is not intended as a substitute for professional legal or accounting advice. The information contained herein may be subject to varying regional and or local differences, laws or regulations.

The purchaser or reader of this publication assumes responsibility for the use of these materials and information.

To Joe's guts!

Praise for this book

"Not only is the buying process explained clearly and fully but Debbie has honed in on the varied towns and cities of the Murcia region to provide painstakingly well-researched information that's invaluable to any prospective buyer."

Martine Cherry
www.dreamspain.net

"Debbie Jenkins impresses again with another invaluable book about Murcia. She has obviously poured countless hours into researching and fine-tuning this invaluable book and her user-friendly format is exactly what you'll need if you're contemplating moving there. There is almost nothing this woman cannot teach you about buying property in Murcia."

Andrea Martins
www.expatwomen.com

"This book is bursting at the seams with the most incredibly well researched and up to date information you'll ever need on buying property in the Murcia region."

Rhiannon Williamson
www.shelteroffshore.com

Contents

PRAISE FOR THIS BOOK
CONTENTS
INTRODUCTION

MURCIA
REGIONAL PROFILE 3
GEOGRAPHY 3
CLIMATE 4
PEOPLE 6
LANGUAGE 7
GETTING THERE 8
GETTING AROUND 10
STANDARD OF LIVING 12
EMPLOYMENT 14
FINANCE & LENDING 16
PROPERTY MARKET 20
IS MURCIA A GOOD INVESTMENT? 20
WHY BUY PROPERTY IN MURCIA? 22
RECENT GROWTH 27
NEW-BUILD PRICES 27

LOCATION, LOCATION, LOCATION
THE LOCATION-O-METER™ 33
AREAS WITHIN THE MURCIA REGION 34
THE NORTH WEST 36
THE NORTH EAST 48
MURCIA 56
THE SOUTH WEST 62
ÁGUILAS & MAZARRÓN 70
CARTAGENA AND THE CAMPO DE CARTAGENA 77
THE MAR MENOR 87

BUYING GUIDE
WHY ARE YOU PLANNING TO BUY HERE? 103
INVESTMENT 103
RETIREMENT 109
RELOCATION 113
HOLIDAY/SECOND HOME 118

WHAT SHOULD YOU BUY? 121
Renovation 121
Self-build 121
New-build and Off-Plan 122
Resale (second hand) 122
Off-Plan versus Second Hand 123

WHERE SHOULD YOU BUY? 128
City 128
Town 130
Countryside 132
Coast/Beach Resort 134
Urbanization/Golf Resort 135

BUYING PROCESS 139
Buying In Murcia - At-A-Glance 139

WHO DOES WHAT? 144
Developer 144
Vendor 144
Estate/Selling Agent 145
Corredor 148
Abogado 148
Gestor 149
Notario 149

ESSENTIALS 152
NIE 152
Bank Account 152
Money 152
Escritura 153
Nota Simple 153
Land Registry 154
Utilities 154
Mortgage 156
Budget Calculator 161
Purchasing a New Build/Off Plan Property 162
Purchasing a Second-Hand/Resale Property 174
TownHouses, Fincas and Rural Properties 184
Building a House 187

VIEWING AND DUE DILIGENCE	**190**
VIEWING	190
PITFALLS	190
WHAT TO LOOK FOR	191
VIEWING CHECKLIST	194
RENTING BEFORE BUYING	195

PROPERTY OWNER'S GUIDE

RENOVATING PROPERTY IN MURCIA	**205**
PERMISSIONS	205
ARCHITECTS	207
FINDING & MANAGING BUILDERS	209
TOOLS AND MATERIALS	210
RENOVATION BUDGET	211
SELLING PROPERTY IN MURCIA	**212**
SELLING YOUR HOUSE	212
SELLER'S TAX LIABILITY	212
TAX DEPOSIT FOR NON-RESIDENT PROPERTY SALES	212
RENTING YOUR PROPERTY IN MURCIA	**213**
BUY TO LET	213
RENTAL LAW IN MURCIA	214
RENTAL TIME PERIODS	215
RENTING YOUR PROPERTY	217
RESOURCES	**218**
ESTATE AGENTS	218
SOLICITORS, LAWYERS & NOTARIES	221
MORTGAGE & FINANCE	221
ACCOUNTANTS	221
CURRENCY EXCHANGE	222
BANKS	222
PROPERTY RENTALS	223
EMPLOYMENT	223
GOVERNMENT	225
NEWSPAPERS, MAGAZINES & JOURNALS	225
RECOMMENDED READING	226
MORE LINKS	226
RELOCATION BUDGET	227
CHANGE OF ADDRESS CHECKLIST	228
ABOUT DEBBIE JENKINS	**229**
PRAISE FOR 'GOING NATIVE IN MURCIA'	237

Introduction

In May 2005 the original *Going Native in Murcia* book was borne out of the frustration of none of the major guides covering the region, or at best only dedicating 4 or 5 pages to it. Since then Murcia has been getting a lot more attention thanks to its wonderful climate, warm and welcoming people and a very strong, and so-far relatively undeveloped, property market.

My husband Marcus and I moved here permanently in late 2005 and started work on the second edition to ensure the content stayed up to date. In 2007 we also set up the *www.nativespain.com* website so everyone else could add to the guide and share their own experiences.

However, it wasn't until my dad asked me to help him look for a house to buy in the region, that I realised *Going Native in Murcia* was lacking. While it gives new residents a great overview of the area including the towns, accommodation, food and activities and even a step-by-step breakdown of the house buying process, it doesn't focus on helping you decide *where in Murcia* to invest your money.

So, this book, *Buying Property in Murcia*, has been written just for you if you want to buy a house, finca, off-plan, castle or cave in the region of Murcia and want the most thoroughly researched information you can get from a buyer's perspective.

My goal is to help both the property investor and the lifestyle buyer alike. A tall order perhaps, but one I think I've achieved successfully with this book. I'll review it, and where necessary update it, each year so I look forward to hearing from you with feedback and ideas.

UPDATES, CHANGES AND YOUR FEEDBACK

We plan to update this book as frequently as possible, to ensure you get the best and most accurate information, probably every year as our publishing budget permits. Publishing a book like this can be quite costly, which is why for this edition I have allowed a select few advertisers to help us cover the costs. We'll see how this works out; let us know your thoughts too.

If you have content for the next edition then get in touch. Perhaps you're a property investor and want to share your strategy, or maybe you've bought off-plan and want to let us know the ins and outs – whatever your circumstances we want to hear your story.

And remember, we're interested in other regions of Spain too, so go to our site and get in touch.

Finally, although inclusion in a book usually implies a recommendation, I cannot list every good business and I apologise in advance if I missed you out - get in touch and let me know. In addition, exclusion does not imply criticism.

> **IMPORTANT**
>
> Whilst all of the information in this guide was as accurate as possible at the time of first publication things do change. Please check for major updates at... *www.nativespain.com*
>
> I'll also post a regular and timely blog on the current property market in Murcia. Stay up to date and post your comments at... *www.nativespain.com/diary/debsjenkins*

MURCIA

ALDRON

Regional Profile

You'd be forgiven for thinking that Murcia contains nothing more than the Mar Menor, La Manga golf club and a swathe of new-build housing estates catering solely for Brits and Germans. This is the view portrayed by most guidebooks and many journalists. Yet it's a view far from reality.

It's true that Murcia does have many golf clubs and an increasing population of northern European immigrants and with 320 days of sunshine per year you can see why. But, it also has mountains, wildlife, a city that retains a unique Spanish culture, unspoilt beaches, national parks, snow (though not much!) and wild boar.

In this section I'll aim to give you a fair and realistic overview of what you can expect in the Murcia region of Spain.

GEOGRAPHY

Murcia, situated on the southeastern corner of Spain, covers 11,000 square kilometres, is made up of 45 municipalities and is home to just over 1 million inhabitants. It sits centrally between the regions of Valencia to the north, La Mancha to the northwest and Andalucía to the west.

The Murcia region is located on the Mediterranean Sea and forms a small sea of its own, known as the Mar Menor. Some of the beaches of the Mar Menor include: San Javier, Santiago de la

The Murcia region is located on the Mediterranean Sea and forms a small sea of its own, known as the Mar Menor.

Ribera, Los Alcázares, and La Manga.

The main city of the region, also called Murcia, lies centrally within the region in a valley along the River Segura. The port of Cartagena, the second largest city in the region, lies on the Costa Cálida

Although Murcia's landscape is generally rugged and arid, there is a wide variety of wildlife and natural beauty including stunning mountains, lush green valleys, sprawling vineyards, pine forests, national parks, salt marshes, rivers, lakes and the only inland sea in Europe.

Murcia has one airport, which although called Murcia airport is actually 50 kilometres (30 miles) from the city of Murcia in the coastal town of San Javier. Another, brand new airport near Corvera to the south of Murcia is still in the planning stages.

CLIMATE

You can enjoy the coast practically year-round in Murcia, from the Easter holidays and well into autumn. There are a great variety of water activities including sailing, windsurfing, water-skiing, scuba diving and kayaking. The average temperature during the year ranges from 11°C in winter to 25°C in summer. The climate is dry and hot in summer and mild in winter. Murcia receives the most sunshine per year in Spain.

The region of Murcia has the typical Mediterranean semi-arid subtropical climate: namely an average annual

Murcia has one airport which is actually 50 km from the city of Murcia in the coastal town of San Javier. A new airport near Corvera is still in the planning stages.

temperature of 18°C, with hot summers (registering peak temperatures of 40°C) and mild winters (though you still might see some snow higher up) with an average temperature of 11°C in the winter months of December and January.

There are between 120-150 days per year with clear skies and 2,800 hours of sun. Rain is scarce throughout the region (approx. 300-350 mm/year), falling mainly in the spring (April) and autumn (October), leaving the summer wonderfully dry. However, due to geography, the temperature differences between the coast and the interior are much more extreme in the winter. On the coast temperatures never tend to fall below 10°C, while inland at higher altitudes (in the Sierra Espuña for example) they may not exceed 6°C. Areas at higher altitude also show a higher average annual rainfall, which reaches 600 mm/yr.

The temperature differences between the coast and the interior are much more extreme in the winter.

month	°C	max day °C	mm/month	days 🌧	days ⚡	days ☁	hours ☀
JAN	10	16	25	3	0	3	170
FEB	12	18	28	3	0	2	180
MAR	13	20	30	3	0	2	210
APR	16	23	27	4	1	1	240
MAY	19	26	32	4	2	1	280
JUN	23	30	20	2	2	1	310
JUL	26	33	5	1	1	0	340
AUG	27	34	10	1	1	0	300
SEP	24	30	27	2	2	1	240
OCT	19	25	44	4	1	1	200
NOV	14	20	32	4	0	2	170
DEC	11	17	21	4	0	3	160
YEAR	18	24	301	35	11	17	2800

PEOPLE

Murcia is a friendly region, a warm "Buenos Dias" upon entering a shop or restaurant is uttered to all, followed by an "Adios" or "Hasta Luego" upon departure. On the coast, they don't expect visitors to speak much Spanish, however in the villages a lack of Spanish can create difficulties as few rural Spaniards learn English.

The Murcianos are a gregarious bunch, taking great care to include children and the older generations in their social activities. They enjoy making an effort in their appearance too; a walk around the Murcian capital on a summer's Saturday evening will show an exuberance of dress that most other westerners generally reserve for weddings! Even the children will be dressed in their finery.

Murcia works on the same timetable as most of the rest of Spain - relaxed! The heat for most of the year encourages a long lunch break, followed by chatting and snoozing during the afternoon siesta. The shops generally close between 2pm and 5pm for most of the year, reopening at 5pm and staying open until 8 or 9 in the evening.

During the hottest months Murcianos take advantage of the cooler evenings, sitting and chatting outside until well past midnight. It's not uncommon to see young children racing round outside restaurants at 2am, while their parents and extended family drink slowly and cool down.

In the villages a lack of Spanish can create difficulties as few rural Spaniards learn English

In August the local Spanish people take a well needed one-month holiday and during this time many shops and restaurants (outside of the tourist destinations) will shut down or work reduced hours, while their Murciano proprietors enjoy the beaches and the mountains.

In addition to the native Spanish population in Murcia you will find the usual pockets of immigrants and expats from the United Kingdom, Ireland, Portugal, Germany, Poland, Eastern Europe, North Africa and many from Latin American countries.

In August many shops and restaurants outside of the tourist destinations will shut down or work reduced hours.

LANGUAGE

The language in Murcia is Castilian Spanish - the standard Spanish you'd be taught in school - and not Catalan.

However, the Spanish spoken in Murcia is quite different from other areas of Spain. "Murciano" tends to eliminate many syllable-final consonants and to emphasise regional vocabulary, much of which is derived from old Arabic words. Some Murcian countryfolk still speak a separate dialect, called Panocho, which is virtually unintelligible to speakers of standard Castilian Spanish.

What you'll most likely notice is the lack of "s" at the end of many words, for example "do" instead "dos" (two).

Language Schools

Instituto Cervantes is an organisation that lists over 1700 Spanish courses in Spain. Take a look here:
http://eee.cervantes.es

The following school in Murcia is also worth trying:

Instituto Hispanico De Murcia

C/ Enrique Villar, 13, 1º B, 30.008 - Murcia (Spain)

☎ 0034 968900325
www.ihdemu.com

Useful Websites

Spanish phrases with audio...
www.quiz-buddy.com/spanish_phrases_with_audio.html

Dictionary...
www.diccionarios.com

Spanish lessons online...
http://en.wikibooks.org/wiki/spanish

Mouse-over words on other websites and get translation and pronounciation...
www.wordchamp.com

"In 1999 141,059 people flew into the San Javier airport, in 2006 that number was 1,645,301 – 11 times more!"

www.carm.es

Airlines...
Jet 2
www.Jet2.com
☎ 902 020051

Ryan Air
www.ryanair.com
☎ 807 220032

Iberia
www.iberia.com
☎ 807 123456

Flybe
www.flybe.com
☎ 0044 13 922 685 28

BMI Baby
www.bmibaby.com
☎ 902 100737

Air Nostrum
www.airnostrum.es
☎ 968 172 045

Air Berlin
www.airberlin.com
☎ 968 172 083

Brussels Airlines
www.brusselsairlines.com
☎ 807 220 003

GETTING THERE

Murcia's only international airport is Murcia-San Javier (MJV), which is located on the Mar Menor coast just south of San Pedro del Pinatar.

However, the regional government has recognised that the 5-jet capacity of the current airport is barely adequate for the 50plus golf complexes that will soon be covering every corner of the region and has approved a plan for a new private airport to be built between Corvera and Valladolises, with a planned completion date of 2010.

However, while the new Corvera airport is in the planning stages, MJV has steadily expanded from its initial single baggage belt in 2003 to 4 in 2005 with another runway built and the terminal and car parking facilities expanded. Despite all this MJV still retains some of its quaint one-horse-town feel and also shares the runway with the local airforce training jets from the Spanish Aeronautical School headed by the King of Spain.

A parking fee was introduced in 2006, so the days of free longterm airport parking are over!

Many of the travellers coming in to Murcia airport stay on the Costa Cálida and do not visit the city of Murcia. The closest train station is in Balsicas. A taxi all the way into Murcia city costs around €60, or you can get a bus (latbus number 73) direct to the city's bus station for €7 (although be aware that there are only 3 buses a day which are all in the evening). *www.aena.es* will allow you to see live arrivals and departures, in English. For those without web access, the telephone number is ☎968 172000.

Destinations include: Barcelona, Madrid, Palma De Mallorca, Helsinki, Dublin, Shannon, Rome, Bergen, Oslo, Trondheim, Birminghan, Glasgow, Leeds, London (Stansted, Gatwick, Luton), Manchester, Manston (Kent), Nottingham, Southampton, Brussels.

The New Airport to the south of Corvera will be closer to the city of Murcia itself and will rival Alicante's El Altet and Málaga for the capacity, duty free shopping and range of fast food franchises. However, as with many projects in the region, it is behind schedule, originally slated to open in 2006, there is still no sign of building, although dozens of golf complexes have sprung up around it in anticipation. It is due for completion in 2010.

Alternative airports for Murcia (in order of convenience) are: Alicante (El Altet), Almería and, if you want the best connectivity, Madrid (Barajas). From Murcia city, with no traffic and with a lead foot, you can get to Alicante in an hour, Almería in two and Madrid in four.

Airlines...
Easyjet
www.easyjet.com
☎ 902 299 992

FlyGlobespan
www.flyglobespan.com
☎ 902 400 069

Jetair Fly
www.jetairfly.com
☎ 968 172 045

Monarch Airlines
www.flymonarch.com
☎ 800 099 260

Norwegian Air Shuttle
www.norwegian.no
☎ 968 172 081

SAS Scandinavian Airlines
www.flysas.es
☎ 807 112 117

Ironically, I noted in the press recently that one of the local golf complexes was complaining to the authorities that they would be in the flight path of the new airport – at the same time as proclaiming proximity to the airport as one of the virtues of buying a house there!

Car Hire Companies...
Centauro
www.centauro.net
☎ 968 572185

Europa
www.europa-rentacar.es
☎ 968 336523

Europ Car
www.europcar.es
☎ 968 335546

Sol Mar
www.solmar.es
☎ 968 335542

As it stands today, Murcia is not particularly well-served by the rail network.

Check timetables and buy tickets at *www.renfe.es*

GETTING AROUND

Car

Murcia has an excellent network of motorways and main roads. Murcia, Águilas, Jumilla, the Mar Menor and Cartagena are all mostly well interlinked. In addition, a new motorway programme is underway to improve the notoriously slow progress around the north of Cartagena, and eventually to link through to Águilas. Be warned that Gatsos (speed cameras) were introduced in Spain in 2005 – and that includes Murcia.

Unless you live full-time in Spain and have bought your own wheels, car rental is probably the most cost-effective way of getting around. For weeklong rentals you can often get a small car for as little as €12 a day.

Rail

As it stands today, Murcia is not particularly well-served by the rail network. You are in luck if you want to travel between Cartegena and Murcia and between Águilas and Murcia but for everywhere else it isn't so good. The train service to Madrid uses the older TALGO/ALTARIA diesel electric trains and so the journey takes some 4 hours. There is also a FEVE line that trundles between Cartagena and Los Nietos (on the Mar Menor near Los Alcázares) – *www.feve.es*.

The super-fast AVE trains (called 'patos' locally) won't be in operation throughout Murcia much before 2010. You can check timetables and buy tickets on the RENFE web site: *www.renfe.es*. Prices are refreshingly reasonable compared to the shocking standard prices in the UK. For example, a return ticket from Murcia to Madrid is currently only €76, and Cartegena to Murcia is €27 return.

Bus

The excellent buses in Murcia make up for the lack of train connections around the region. From Murcia's main bus station you can get to just about anywhere in the country.

Most long distance routes are serviced by the ALSA bus company: *www.alsa.es*

If you wanted to go to Málaga by train, you would have to go almost all the way into Madrid and then back down south to the coast. In contrast there are buses from Murcia going straight there. The long-distance coaches are good value, for example a return ticket from Murcia to Madrid is just €43.

However, the services between outlying towns could hardly be called frequent. For example, there are only 3 buses a day during the week from Fuente Álamo into Murcia and none on Sunday. However, if you do ever see such a bus, the journey would only cost you €2.20.

For buses around the region you can try Latbus ☎ ☐968 250088 and *www.latbus.com*

Taxi

In Murcia or Cartagena, assuming you don't want to walk, a taxi can be a reasonable option. You want to look for taxis from a taxi rank or one that you have phoned in advance.

Taxis are certainly very reasonably priced per kilometre but as soon as you start getting out of the city the kilometres quickly mount up. There are plenty of travellers who have bagged a bargain basement flight to 'Murcia' and then caught a cab into town only to find that it would probably have been cheaper to hire a car for the whole weekend.

STANDARD OF LIVING

The days when prices for everything in Spain were incredibly cheap compared to the UK are long gone and now you can expect to pay a similar amount for most things as you'd expect to pay in the rest of Europe. However, some things – such as cigarettes, alcohol, eating out and fresh food – are still exceptionally good value in Spain.

Our last three course evening meal for three people, with drinks beforehand, wine with the meal and coffees etc, totalled just €60. That's just fifteen pounds each! The daytime set menu can be as low as €7 per person.

The region of Murcia covers an area of just over 11,000 sq km, with a population of a little over 1 million – that's just 110 people per sq km compared to the UK's 383.

Cost of Living Comparison

	BRITAIN	MURCIA
BOTTLE OF RED WINE	£5.00	£2.00
PINT OF LAGER	£2.50	£1.50
PACKET OF CIGARETTES	£4.00	£1.00
3KM TAXI JOURNEY	£5.00	£3.00
3 COURSE DINNER FOR 2 (WITH WINE)	£50.00	£30.00
LITRE OF PETROL	90p	60p

The following graph shows the comparative prive levels between Spain, UK and France. Comparative price levels are the ratio between Purchasing power parities (PPPs) and market exchange rate for each country. PPPs are currency conversion rates that convert economic indicators expressed in national currencies to a common currency, called Purchasing Power Standard (PPS), which equalises the purchasing power of different national currencies and thus allows meaningful comparison. The ratio is shown in relation to the EU average (EU27 = 100). If the index of the comparative price levels shown for a country is higher or lower than 100, the country concerned is relatively expensive or cheap as compared with the EU average.

Comparatively speaking it is cheaper to live in Spain.

Comparative Price Levels
based on final consumption by private households (EU-27 = 100)

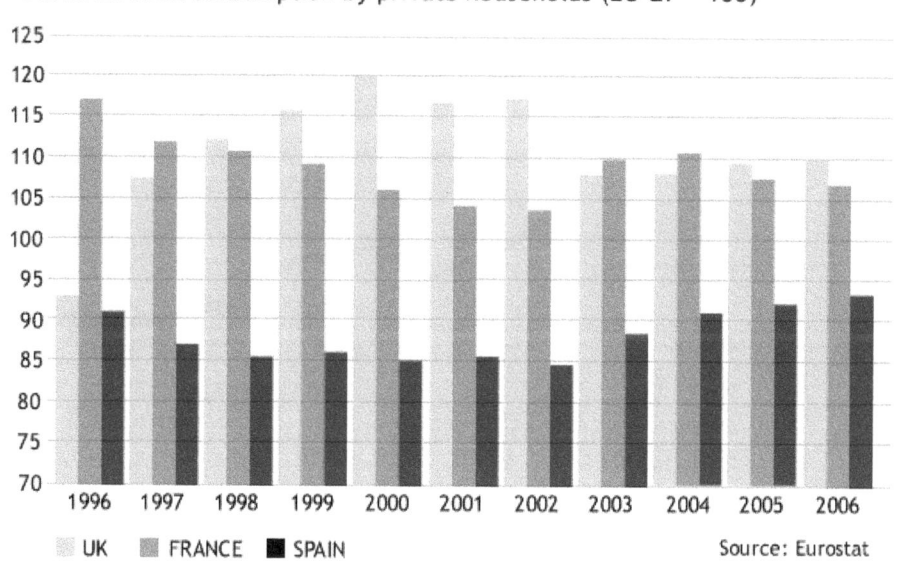

Source: Eurostat

EMPLOYMENT

The 2006 Fundación de las Cajas de Ahorros (Funcas) study, which looks at economic growth within all the Spanish regions, identified the evolution of regional economies throughout Spain over the last 7 years and according to the results Murcia saw the highest growth in GDP per inhabitant at 4.14%. With the average growth in GDP per inhabitant at 3.2% in Spain.

Over the last 7 years Murcia saw the highest growth in GDP per inhabitant.

The unemployment rate, taken from International Labour Office (ILO) definition (unemployment rate represents unemployed persons as a percentage of the labour force) is currently at 8.1%. This is a little higher than the rate for the EU, 7.3%. However, it does show a dramatic downward trend. Note using the same source of data the UK is shown at 5.3% unemployment.

Plummeting Unemployment

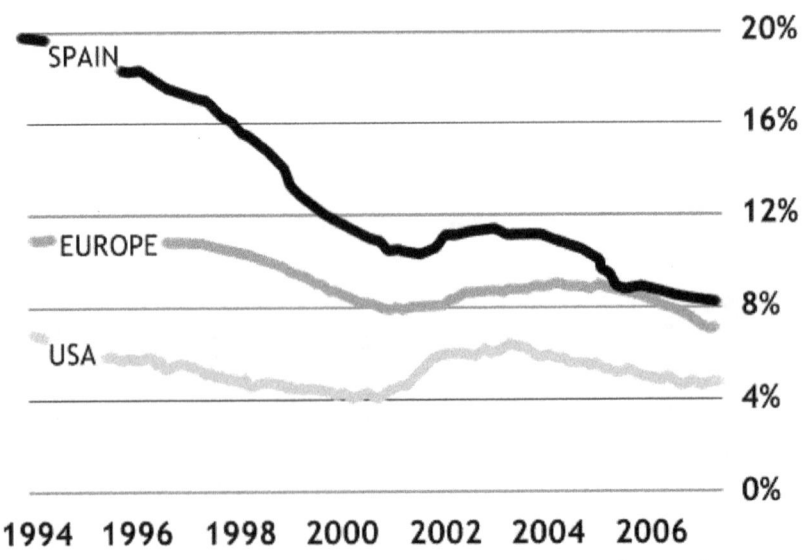

Source: Eurostat

The following data was extracted (with a little pain!) from *www.ine.es* - the Spanish Government facts and figures website.

There are few large employers in the region, just 44 employing more than 500 salaried workers. The vast majority of the almost 107,000 companies in the region employ 2 or fewer people (around 70%). Of those larger companies they tend to be in the mineral and oil extraction and processing businesses, transportation and automotive, ship building and chemicals.

There are 1,318 businesses in food and drink production, 509 in the manufacture of furniture, 1,446 in metallic manufacturing, 951 making metallic machines for the construction industry, a few thousand making general machinery, 8,500 in hostelry, hotels and restaurants, around 12,000 in the transportation fields, a growing 4,000 in finances, pensions and securities and a whopping 16,000 businesses in the real estate market.

Interestingly there are 16,651 businesses in the construction industry, with another 10,000 businesses supporting them in the civil engineering field and 7,000 in the buildings and works facilities industry. There's big business in transporting things by pipe, with almost 6,000 employers.

In IT there are just over 1,000 businesses, 1,500 in education, 2,000 in recreation, culture and sport and over 11,000 in the "other" category.

The total number of businesses has risen from a little over 74,000 in 1999 to almost 107,000 in 2007.

The total number of businesses has risen from a little over 74,000 in 1999 to almost 107,000 in 2007. That's a rise of 30% in 8 years against a national rise of 24% (2.8 million in 1999 to 3.7 million in 2007) in the same period.

FINANCE & LENDING

Spain's financial sectors are diverse, modern, and fully integrated into international financial markets. Spain has 348 credit entities, including private banks, savings banks, credit unions, finance houses, and branches of foreign banks headquartered in non-EU countries. Two large private commercial banks, Banco Santander Central Hispano and Banco Bilbao Vizcaya Argentaria, dominate the banking sector and account for over half of Spain's banking assets. Sixty-one foreign banks together account for less than 15 per cent of total banking assets. The government also provides subsidised financing through several modest credit institutions.

Mortgages on Urban Properties[1]

	TOTAL URBAN		HOUSES		LAND		OTHER	
	No.	'000s of Euros	No.	'000s of Euros	No.	'000s of Euros	No.	'000s of Euros
2003	46,611	3,618,331	35,726	2,679,637	1,223	314,334	9,661	624,321
2004	59,734	5,352,679	42,323	3,844,149	1,247	392,511	16,167	1,116,006
2005	69,208	7,767,153	50,602	5,347,240	2,010	751,053	16,596	1,668,860
2006	72,837	8,669,265	54,526	6,419,980	1,700	732,468	16,611	1,516,817

---

[1] Data from INES.es

Mortgage Providers for Rustic Properties

	RUSTIC PROPERTY		BANKS		SAVINGS BANKS		OTHERS	
	No.	'000s of Euros	No.	'000s of Euros	No.	'000s of Euros	No.	'000s of Euros
2003	2,495	304,624	464	67,430	1,638	196,485	399	40,675
2004	3,092	604,773	655	199,056	1,998	344,374	440	61,323
2005	3,315	914,423	629	313,571	2,212	509,966	474	90,881
2006	3,336	1,223,946	669	275,210	2,051	692,889	616	255,847

The number of mortgages on urban properties has risen in the 4 years from 2003 to 2006, though the pace of increase has slowed. In 2006 over 8.6 Billion Euros was owed in mortgages on properties.

The majority of mortgages in Spain are taken out with Savings Banks (Cajas de Ahorros). Again there have been rises in the numbers of mortgages over this 4-year period.

Mortgage rates are calculated as Euribor plus the bank rate. You can see in the following chart that the Euribor was at its lowest rate during 2003, 2004 and 2005 and has seen steady increases over the last 2 years, not quite reaching the peak of 2002. This means the cost of borrowing is higher now than in 2005 and many people have found themselves with an ever-increasing mortgage.

The Euro Interbank Offered Rate (or Euribor) is a daily reference rate based on the averaged interest rates at which banks offer to lend unsecured funds to other banks in the euro wholesale money market (or interbank market).

Spain's Euribor Rate

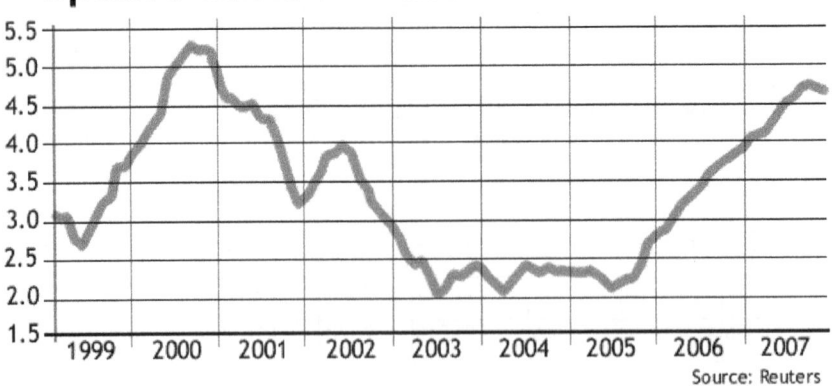

Source: Reuters

MIGRATION

The table shows the massive increase in immigration in the region over the last few years, with data being available upto 2006. The data is from CREM (the website is *www.carm.es*) and shows the numbers of people registering on the padrón. The numbers of actual immigrants are almost certainly much higher than shown as many don't register. The majority of immigrants are centred around the cities, for example Murcia, Cartagena and Lorca, with Mazarrón close behind.

	Numbers			
	2000	2002	2004	2006
REGIÓN OF MURCIA	22,995	83,546	132,918	189,053
Abanilla	117	222	304	567
Abarán	121	627	899	1,065
Águilas	664	1,592	2,548	4,038
Albudeite	1	6	13	27
Alcantarilla	229	1,091	2,072	3,083
Alcázares (Los)	926	1,942	3,408	4,843
Aledo	5	29	68	84
Alguazas	51	274	529	1,042

Alhama de Murcia	369	1,103	1,993	2,825
Archena	121	971	1,503	2,115
Beniel	156	794	1,298	1,864
Blanca	88	170	313	436
Bullas	45	378	541	817
Calasparra	17	304	682	1,003
Campos del Río	19	67	77	140
Caravaca de la Cruz	212	1,049	1,646	2,389
Cartagena	3,537	9,615	17,447	26,605
Cehegín	57	356	667	1,216
Ceutí	51	347	565	806
Cieza	309	1,173	1,763	2,538
Fortuna	90	393	732	1,464
Fuente-Álamo	673	2,352	3,525	4,428
Jumilla	377	2,496	3,289	3,582
Librilla	31	77	143	235
Lorca	1,680	8,602	12,948	17,923
Lorquí	58	349	621	884
Mazarrón	1,869	5,648	8,357	12,441
Molina de Segura	644	2,808	4,605	6,982
Moratalla	24	169	262	216
Mula	53	1,143	1,679	2,207
Murcia	4,630	19,305	33,227	46,344
Pliego	24	51	127	311
Puerto-Lumbreras	155	603	1,009	1,581
Ricote	17	30	35	57
San Javier	431	2,710	4,864	7,052
San Pedro del Pinatar	345	1,634	2,689	4,627
Santomera	344	970	1,294	1,935
Torre-Pacheco	2,673	4,998	5,500	6,460
Torres de Cotillas (Las)	277	628	1,030	1,573
Totana	678	3,380	4,268	5,695
Ulea	16	23	28	33
Unión (La)	333	641	919	1,441
Villanueva del Río Segura	7	21	49	68
Yecla	471	2,405	3,382	4,011

The majority of immigrants are centred around the cities, for example Murcia, Cartagena and Lorca, with Mazarrón close behind.

Property Market

IS MURCIA A GOOD INVESTMENT?

Only you can decide. Each person is investing their hard-earned cash for a different reason. Weigh up the pros and cons, talk to professionals, get advice from others who've come before you and, of course, take a quick look into your crystal ball before deciding. Here are the extremes of opinion along with my own view.

An Optimistic Outlook

House prices have rocketed in the past in this region for a reason - the location is great, the infrastructure is improving, there are still plenty of opportunities and the prices have been low.

However, the figures suggest that Murcia is still undervalued compared to other markets including other areas of Spain and especially emerging markets in Eastern Europe.

A major "property price correction" might hit other *overvalued* areas but will leave Murcia pretty much unharmed. So while the days of huge and fast profits may be numbered in many areas annual growth prospects are still very promising.

A Pessimistic Outlook

The house price bubble, which has been growing at a frightening rate, could burst at any moment. Developers are creating an oversupply of lower quality properties. Sales are slowing...

While the days of huge and fast profits may be numbered in many areas annual growth prospects are still very promising.

growth is slowing... some developers are feeling the pinch already... it's just a matter of time... And if the bubble *does* burst there will be a lot of ordinary people, stuck with properties that are falling in value.

A Balanced Outlook?

I long ago ditched my mom's advice - "If you don't have anything nice to say say nothing at all" - and I've hopefully given you a warts and all account of the region with this book.

I must say, however, that I'm still very positive about the prospects of growth here, especially over the longer (10 years plus) term.

So who's most wrong? The optimist or the pessimist? Only time will tell but my best guess, and my own strategy, is to invest for the longer term and avoid overstretching yourself by using strategies that rely too heavily on the same market growth Murcia has enjoyed in the recent past.

Going for large and quick profit, which you could have achieved easily just a few years ago, is a gamble at the moment. You need a strong stomach for the risk and deep pockets if things go wrong.

Unless you buy below market value and add value through renovation there's a chance of your investment reducing in value, at least for the short term.

It's a buyer's market right now so there are plenty of chances to buy smart and make a long-term profit. If you're buying renovation properties in towns then the effects of over building

If the bubble bursts a lot of people could be stuck with properties that are falling in value.

Unless you buy below market value there's a risk of your investment reducing in value - at least for the short term.

> "Grupo I's latest report puts annual demand for new holiday homes in Spain at about 90,000, yet 140,000 are built each year, which means the stock of unsold properties must be growing. Furthermore, 80% of developers recently surveyed by Grupo i reported that sales were worse or much worse, while 77% had a negative or very negative outlook."
>
> Sunday Times, October 2007

on new resorts will have less of an impact. If you're buying on a new development however, then buy carefully and ensure you're getting a property that isn't overpriced.

WHY BUY PROPERTY IN MURCIA?

As you're reading this book you've most probably already decided that you will be buying somewhere in Murcia and there is no need for me to try to convince you that your decision is a good one. So, what I've done instead is to highlight the main reasons why you're not alone in your decision to invest here.

Attractive Property Prices and Promising Capital Gain Prospects

While house prices continue to grow in the region, meaning fewer bargains than were available just a few years ago, you can still get quite a lot of house for your money here and capital growth prospects remain positive as the region develops.

For example our land and small house purchase in 2002 for £20,000 is now worth around £100,000. One of our Spanish neighbours has recently sold a parcel of land for £200,000, which 5 years ago was worth just £50,000.

It's Currently a Buyer's Market

There are 50 proposed golf courses in the region with 14 already built or being built so there are plenty of buying options and plenty of bargains to be had.

Even with the recent rapid growth of property prices in the last few years, this area is still relatively virgin territory. Getting in early with this young market is sure to yield long term gains as have been seen in other areas of Spain.

A negative side-effect of all this new building from a seller's perspective is that there is an oversupply of new property in some (mostly resort/urbanisation) areas. The good news for you as a buyer is that puts you in a strong bargaining position and you'd be mad not to haggle on price.

Compared to most of the rest of Spain, however, Murcia property is still massively undervalued – although it's catching up – so even taking into account a major market correction (drop in house prices) for Spain in general, long term prospects for prices in the region are good.

Quarterly House Price Trends

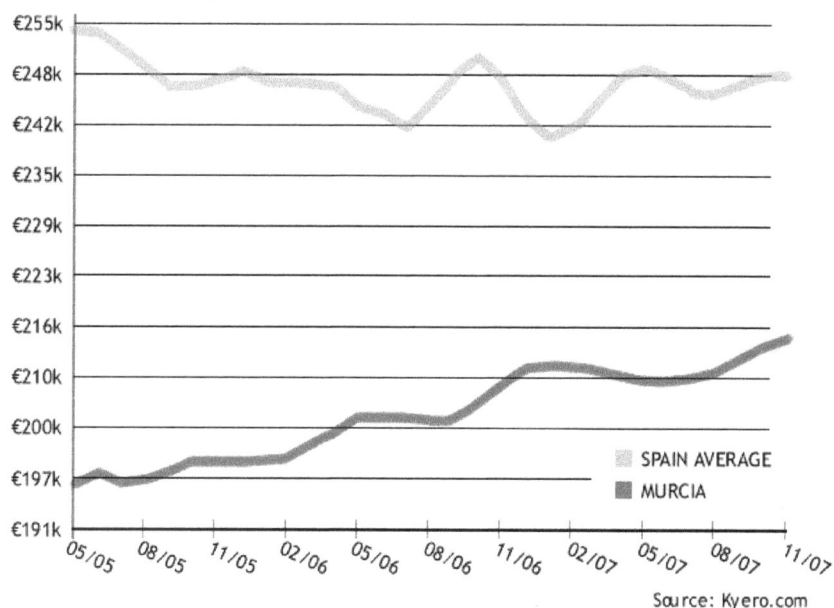

Source: Kyero.com

A consortium led by Sacyr Vallehermoso has been awarded the contract to build and run the new international airport in Corvera which is scheduled to open in 2010.

Sacyr said the consortium will invest €555 million. The overall budget for the airport is now at €185 million.

Due to an enormous increase of tourism in Murcia it is estimated that 1.5 million passengers will fly into the Murcia region in the opening year of the airport, and about 675 jobs will be created.

Plenty of New Developments and Infrastructure Improvements

The government's intention to achieve adequate housing for all citizens, the sustainable development of land and rehabilitating neighbourhoods means there will be more internal investment over the coming years.

While the new Corvera airport lingers in the planning stage, San Javier airport is being expanded as tourism in the area increases. The increased aiport service and prospect of even better access once Corvera is complete is another reason why house prices are still increasing and more golf developments are springing up.

Murcia already has a great motorway network, which has been extended with an east-west link bypassing Cartagena and linking through to Mazarrón and Águilas. In addition there's also the new road from Mazarron to Lorca.

The government plans to link Murcia up to the high-speed national rail network, called AVE trains. This should be complete by 2010 to Murcia city, ensuring trips from Murcia to Madrid will be reduced from 4 hours to just 2.5 hours.

Greater water capacity, one of the greatest challenges in the past for this area (and a reason why development here originally lagged behind some other areas of Spain), is being provided through new desalination plants.

Murcia also has 18 hospitals, four international schools and three universities. Murcia University was founded more than 700 years ago, making it one of the oldest in Europe.

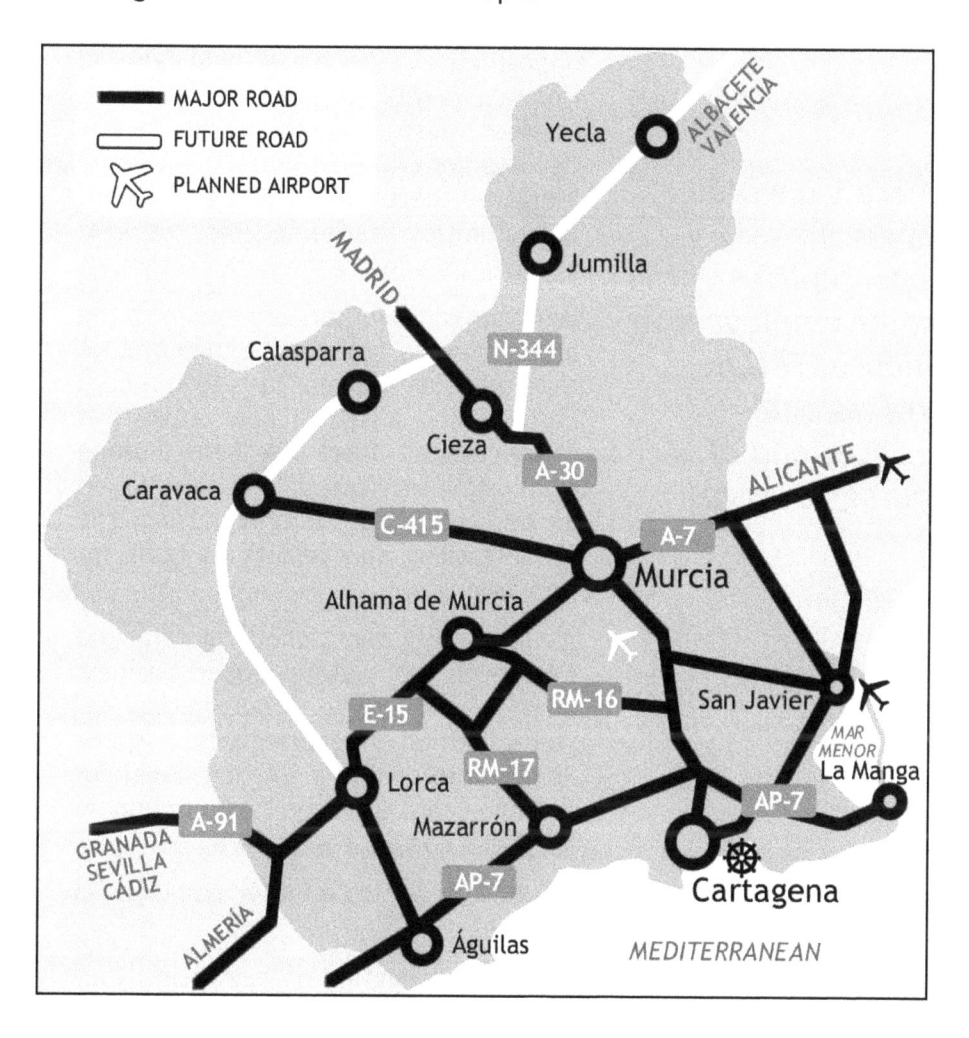

Employment Prospects

Murcia's main source of prosperity has traditionally been from agriculture although in the main cities of Cartagena and Murcia itself you can expect to find a wide range of opportunities with major employers in finance, retail and professional services. Also, thanks to the recent development of Murcia's tourist industry, there is a growing range of opportunities in the leisure, tourism, construction and real estate sectors.

Many migrant workers are drawn to the area, from as far afield as Mexico, to take on tough manual jobs (often on a cash-in-hand basis) in agriculture and many expats from Western Europe offer their services to one another, in a kind of mini-economy, using the urbanizations and resorts as hubs for networking.

As previously mentioned, Murcia and Cartagena are well-developed business cities, with many opportunities for well-qualified people who speak Spanish to earn a higher level of income than is likely to be found in rural and coastal resort areas.

GE Plastics is also a major employer in the area.

If you are planning on relocating your business or yourself to Murcia then lack of internet access isn't a barrier to "home working" as ADSL has now reached most towns here.

There's a wide range of opportunities with major employers in finance, retail, professional services and of course Tourism.

RECENT GROWTH

Murcia is one of the few regions in Spain that still has steady growth in house prices. The latest government figures (July 2007) indicate that there has been an increase of 9.5% in the last 12 months for the Murcia region, set against an average National rise of just 5.8%.

	2005-03	2005-04	2006-01	2006-02	2006-03	2006-04	2007-01	2007-02	2007-03
SPAIN	€249k	€247k	€247k	€244k	€245k	€247k	€242k	€248k	€246k
MURCIA	€197k	€199k	€200k	€204k	€204k	€209k	€211k	€209k	€210k

Source: Kyero.com

Data from the popular (and very good) Kyero.com website suggests the same as the government figures, with house prices in Murcia still rising slightly compared to the national average, though perhaps not so optimistically. It also shows that Murcia is still a relatively inexpensive place to buy compared to the national average.

Take a look on www.Kyero.com for up to date statistics on the housing market.

NEW-BUILD PRICES

Here are the latest average prices for new build properties in Murcia itself. These figures are based on recent valuations carried out by Sociedad de Tasación. The most expensive areas are still found around the coast, with Cartagena, San Javier and San Pedro del Pinatar taking the lead. It's also still relatively expensive to buy in the city of Murcia. Lowest cost houses are found inland with some of the cheapest new builds in the North East around Yecla and Jumilla.

Region/ Province	Price €/m²	Annual % change
Cartagena	1,740	8.7%
Jumilla	1,132	8.8%
Lorca	1,375	9.1%
Mazarron	1,492	8.6%
Murcia	1,613	7.4%
San Javier	1,720	9.6%
San Pedro	1,695	7.3%
Yecla	1,290	11.2%

This league table shows average property inflation rates and average property prices in €/m² for a selection of Spanish regions.

Region/Province	Price €/m²	Annual % change
Granada	1,470.7	9.9%
Extremadura	1,020.1	9.6%
Murcia	1,578.3	9.5%
Tarragona	1,875.3	8.7%
Cadiz	1,856.2	8.4%
Cordoba	1,516.4	7.9%
Balearics	2,364.6	7.8%
Galicia	1,512.2	7.5%
Valencia	1,564.8	7.3%
Asturias	1,727.4	7.2%
Girona	2,119.6	7.1%
Almeria	1,618.1	7.1%
Andalusia	1,740.4	7.0%
Cantabria	2,030.7	6.5%
Seville	1,702.6	6.3%
Las Palmas	1,843.9	6.0%
Canaries	1,797.6	6.0%
Tenerife	1,733.8	5.8%
Catalonia	2,382.3	5.6%
Castellon	1,739.4	5.6%
Barcelona	2,684.5	5.2%
Valencia	1,649.5	5.0%
Malaga	2,270.0	3.9%
Teruel	996.9	3.5%
Madrid	2,989.1	3.0%
Alicante	1,737.4	2.1%

Mark Stucklin's Analysis for Q2 2007

According to the government's figures, 'emerging' regions such as Granada, Extremadura and Murcia are still growing robustly at close to 10%, whilst traditional destinations such as Malaga and Alicante have fallen to the bottom of the table. This is a reversal of the situation in 2003, when Malaga and Alicante were two of the strongest regions, with price increases of over 20%. High prices and over development in traditional areas have pushed buyers to new regions.

Taking the government's figures at face value, it appears that property prices are still increasing at between 5% and 10% in most popular areas, with the exception of Malaga and Alicante. Note that the general consumer inflation rate in Spain is 2.4%, so real price increases are reduced by this amount. After adjusting for inflation, real property prices are falling slightly in Alicante, and only increasing by 1.5% in Malaga.

Stucklin's analysis goes on to suggest that there is a real risk of a "soft landing" in the Spanish housing market. With concerns over the ever-increasing mortgage interest rates and the possibility of a construction-led recession (due to

If you're serious about buying property in Spain you really should register for Stucklin's free newsletter

www.spanishpropertyinsight.com

more than 18% of Spanish GDP being housing related) he advises caution in Spain.

However, as mentioned earlier, this also means it is a buyer's market and if you're in it for the long return then good investments can still be found.

Stucklin goes on to say *"Price differentials between the pockets of quality and the rest are likely to increase, with quality property rising in value, whilst the rest of the market stagnates at best."*

Which leads the way for savvy buyers to seek out high quality properties at reasonable prices.

LOCATION, LOCATION, LOCATION

The Location-o-Meter™

The Location-o-Meter™ is your at-a-glance guide to each town and the major areas.

PROPERTY PRICES - a high number indicates higher prices.

PROPERTY AVAILABILITY - a high number indicates that there are plenty of properties available in this area.

RENTAL MARKET - a higher number suggests more opportunities for tourist rental or long-term rental where indicated.

TRANSPORT LINKS - the higher the number the better the transport access and infrastructure, including roads, airports, trains and public transport.

INFRASTRUCTURE - this covers local amenities including health centres, schools, shopping, restaurants and bars. Higher numbers mean access and availability of essential infrastructure is high.

DEVELOPMENTS/PLANNING - a high number indicates that there are lots of new developments, urbanisations and houses in the planning stage or already being built.

EXPAT-O-METER - the more expats in an area the higher the number! We'll let you decide if that's a good thing or not!

There's no "judgement" inherent in the numbers given, as some people will be happy with lots of development and others will not - it's just a scale.

It's designed to give you a quick overview so you can see if a town or area is right for you.

Areas within the Murcia Region

Remember this split of the region is arbitrary and there is some overlapping.

It's difficult, without over generalising, to split the region up into smaller sections. However, by doing this, you'll get more quickly to the heart of each area with exceptions being pointed out. So for the purpose of this guide the region has been subdivided as follows:

- The North West – including Caravaca de la Cruz, Moratalla, Cehegín, Calasaparra, Bullas and Mula.
- The North East – including Jumilla, Yecla, Ricote Valle, Archena and Fortuna.
- Murcia – including the city and its surrounding suburbs.
- The South West – including Alhama, Totana, Aledo, Lorca and Sierra Espuña.
- Águilas & Mazarron – including Águilas, Mazarron and Puerto Mazarron
- Cartagena and the Campo de Cartagena – including Fuente Álamo, Balsicas, Corvera and the city of Cartagena.
- The Mar Menor – all areas bordering on the Mar Menor coast including San Pedro del Pinatar, San Javier, Los Alcázares and La Manga.

The Campo de Cartagena has seen the majority of new developments in the last 10 or so years, with several new resorts being built.

NativeSpain.com

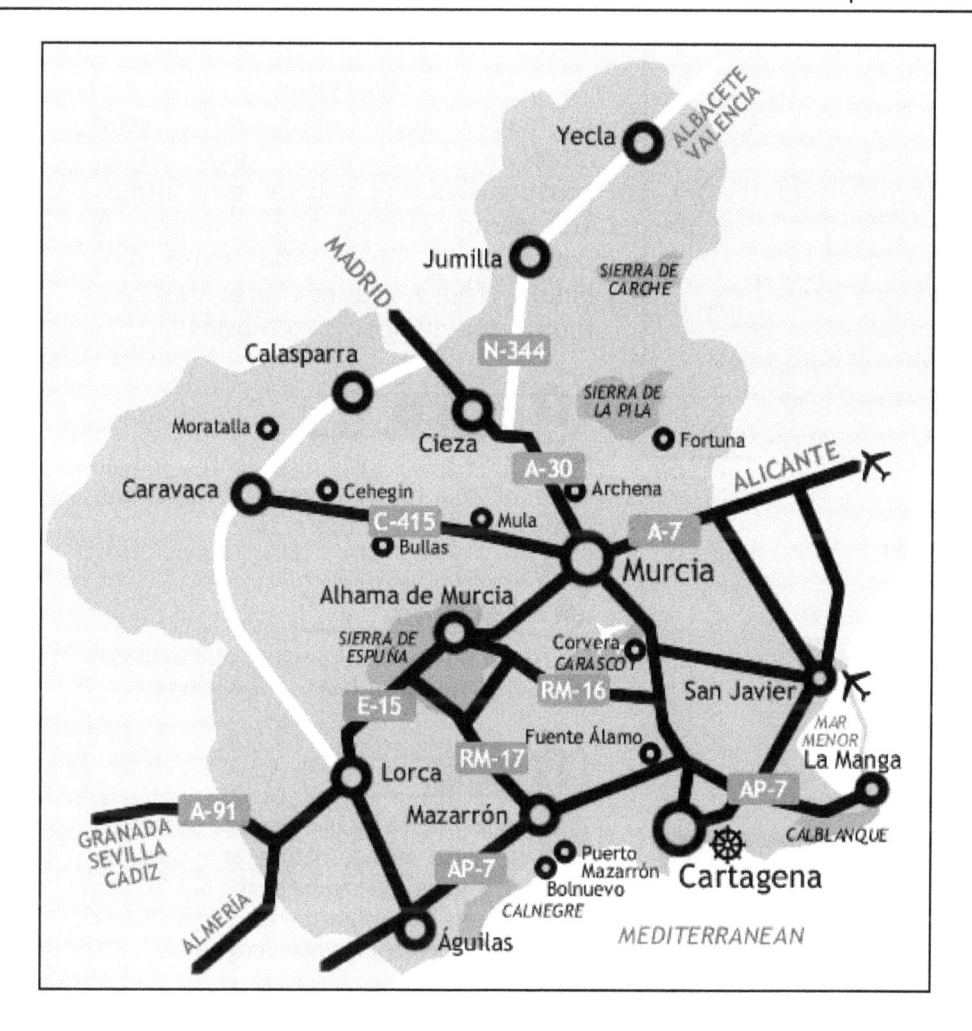

Buying Property in Murcia

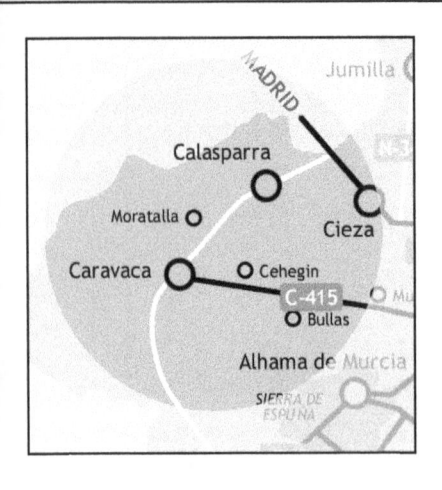

THE NORTH WEST

Overview

A mainly rural area, with good motorway access, and small communities and villages on hilltops. The campo around these villages is dotted with fincas and some new builds. There are few urbanisations, though the number is increasing.

PROPERTY PRICES

Prices have been going up recently, though some of the most economical purchases can still be found in this area.

PROPERTY AVAILABILITY

There are plenty of reforms available in the old towns, fincas and new developments.

RENTAL MARKET

The stunning Sierra Espuña regional park offers walking, horse riding, nature and camping. Within 1.5 hours you can be at the beach. This area appeals to rural tourists with tourist rental being more viable than long-term.

TRANSPORT LINKS

Good motorway access is due to get better over the next 5 years. Between 1 and 2 hours from the nearest airports.

INFRASTRUCTURE

Whilst the area has been growing in popularity it still relies on access to Murcia city for many of its main health requirements. All the towns have adequate health and education facilities.

DEVELOPMENT/PLANNING

More developments are springing up, although they appear to be well thought out and fairly slow to come to fruition.

EXPAT-O-METER

Relatively late to the expat market, there are some noticeable exceptions. Cehegín, for example, has a thriving expat community.

Developments in the North West

A mostly undeveloped area, the majority of recent new builds have been around the main towns and for resident Spanish purchasers. The small number of golf and tourist urbanisations are new for this area.

El Balcón de Moratalla is a new development of villas, flats and bungalows
www.elbalcondemoratalla.es

Lomas de Moratalla is a development of luxury detached villas and rural townhouses with pools, green space, commercial and leisure areas. *www.lomasdemoratalla.co.uk*

Las Higuericas Finca Parcs on the Murcia/Albacete border has a completion date of between 2008 and 2010. The developers are Dragados, see *www.fincaparcs.com* for more details.

There are three newer developments in Calasparra - Cañada Verde, Coto Rinales and Tierra de Sol. Then there's the more developed Las Torrentes estate in Calasparra.

In Caravaca de la Cruz there is Nature which is set for completion in 2009

Developers

www.elbalcondemoratalla.es
www.lomasdemoratalla.co.uk
www.fincaparcs.com
www.grupotrampolin.com

If you own or know of a development that isn't mentioned here please go to *www.NativeSpain.com* and add it for inclusion in the next edition.

with a planned 3000 homes and Trampolin in Mula (*www.grupotrampolin.com*) with 2700 properties, 400 of which are apartments. Recently one of the development partners (Llanera) has had financial problems and has withdrawn from the partnership.

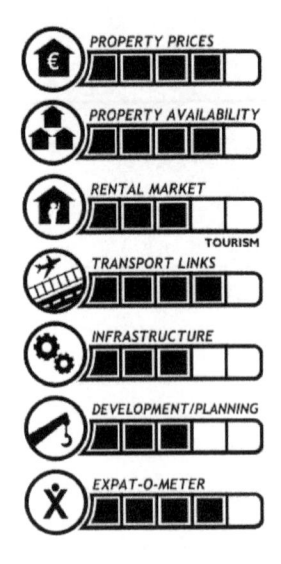

Bullas

Population: 11,000

Bullas is one of the five towns (along with Calasparra, Caravaca de la Cruz, Cehegín and Moratalla) which makes up the area called Comarca del Noroeste – the natural access to the North East of the region. This area has a relative abundance of water making for more agriculture and pine forest growth.

There are two parts to the town including the ancient part with winding streets where you can get your car wedged and the newer area where younger Spanish residents live, work and socialise.

You can pick up a vineyard (they make great wine around here) for a cool €345,000, a townhouse in need of renovation for less than €50,000, reformed townhouses for less than €100,000 and large fincas for around €300,000.

Their fiesta is in October, starting the night of the Friday before the first Sunday of October and finishing on the following Tuesday. There is also a fiesta on the 17th January, San Antón (La Copa).

PROPERTY PRICES

PROPERTY AVAILABILITY

RENTAL MARKET

TOURISM

TRANSPORT LINKS

INFRASTRUCTURE

DEVELOPMENT/PLANNING

EXPAT-O-METER

Ayuntamiento - Plaza de España
☎ 968 652031

www.bullas.net - this is one of the best local websites in the region, perhaps in the whole of Spain! You'll find a lot of tourist information on this site too.

Spanglish and Loving It

I'm Lisa Hodgkiss from Devon. I moved to Bullas in 2003 with my family.

We were always going to retire to Spain but, when house prices in Devon shot up and doubled, we decided to bring our plans forward and take the plunge.

We went on the internet in the UK to look and found what we thought was the best website - *www.noblevalera.com*. The prices were listed, properties were well-photographed and described and we contacted them and arranged to fly over to check out some properties listed with them. To be perfectly truthful, back in 2002 for the Murcia inland region, they were about the only website worth looking at. Friends of ours had moved out to Lorca in Murcia in September 2002 and so we thought we, too, would check it out.

We now live in the campo near Bullas with 1½ acres land with fruit and olive trees. There are a couple of houses dotted around so we are not isolated but you can't pop your head over the fence to ask for a cup of sugar either!

We left absolutely bugger all behind unless you count family - who lived over 3 hours away anyway!

I am the editor of The North West Murcia Gazette. I started it back in November 2004 as the first magazine in the North West Murcia area. Now, 3 years on, it is a glossy colour monthly magazine and it has been used as a "blueprint" for others. There are a large number of people who subscribe to the magazine both here in Spain and in the UK and adverts come from as far afield as Malaga. There is a fabulous website to accompany the magazine - *www.murciagazette.com*

We have been extremely lucky in that we both have our own businesses and they are doing well. We have all that we could ever have wished for (and more) so our plan is to carry on as we are – for the foreseeable future at least.

In my experience the biggest mistake people make is not checking out the area for work availability and cost of living; it's not as cheap here in Spain as it used to be.

And people shouldn't come here thinking it is hot all year round - you *will* need heaters in the winter. Also, bear in mind that wages in Murcia are the lowest for the whole of Spain so you can expect to earn around €5-7 per hour even if you are "qualified". Electricity and telephone bills here are expensive too.

The best thing about living here is the fantastic views, the peace and quiet and the friendly Bullas people. I have loads of space for my 3 dogs (a German Shepherd, a Boxer and an English Bulldog) and my Blue and Gold Macaw.

However, Bullas is quite backward in many ways. It is similar to what the UK was like perhaps when my grandparents were young. I do not mean this in a derogatory way but even the Bulleros say themselves "we are simple people." Sometimes it can be very frustrating when nobody seems to know what they are doing (I know Spain in general can be very "mañana" but it is much worse here in Bullas). I also get very upset at the number of stray animals here and the treatment of animals in general but I knew all that before I came to live here.

I think it's extremely important to be able to speak Spanish. However, it was easier when we moved here as we were the first English family in Bullas so had no choice but to learn. Now Brits come over and only mix with other Brits and I think that is quite sad.

The only thing I miss is Christmas in the UK. I cannot get used to it here, even though I would not fly home for it. I have chosen to live here and so it is one of those things that I will get used to I am sure.

And in case you didn't know, Bullas wine is fantastic! There is a brilliant wine museum which is well worth a visit and there are lots of great places to eat and bars that specialise in seafood.

I have no regrets whatsoever. I love it here!

Calasparra

Population: 9,300

Prices range from €400,000+ for a villa on the new Las Torrentas development to fincas for around €150,000 in the surrounding countryside. Townhouses sell for around €150,000 and you'll get apartments for less than €100,000 on the Tierra De Sol urbanisation.

Calasparra is noted for its excellent rice growing, which is due to the proximity of the rivers Segura, Quípar and Argos. In the centre of town you can find the remains of an Arab castle off Plaza de la Constitución. There is an archaeological museum in the old Palace House of La Encomienda and there are a number of old churches such as Iglesia de la Merced, Iglesia de san Pedro (18th century) and Iglesia de los Santos (18th century).

Around Calasparra you can go up to Las Lomas de la Virgen to get a fantastic view of the mountains, the river and the rice fields. Nearby you'll find the natural reserve of Cañadaverosa. Calasparra has a fiesta of Virgen de la Esperanza which is between the 2nd and 8th of September.

Calasparra rice is the first in the world to have been awarded a "Denominación de Origen" – DOC, which symbolises a guarantee of high quality. The rice is grown in a special environment – both sunny and mountainous, ranging from 340 to 500 metres in altitude, and irrigated with fresh water from the river Segura.

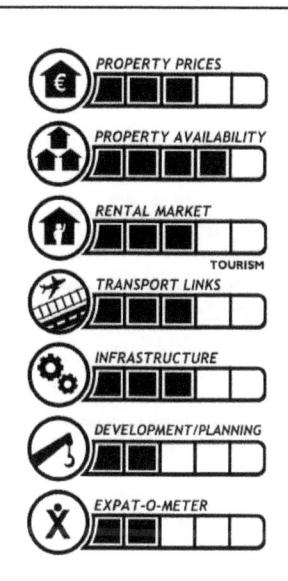

- PROPERTY PRICES
- PROPERTY AVAILABILITY
- RENTAL MARKET
- TRANSPORT LINKS — TOURISM
- INFRASTRUCTURE
- DEVELOPMENT/PLANNING
- EXPAT-O-METER

Calasparra specialities such as rice, sweets and cheeses can be found in Calle Teniente Flomesta.

Tourist Office – San Abdón, 15
☎ 968 723000

Ayuntamiento – Plaza Corredera, 27
☎ 968 720044
www.foro-ciudad.com/murcia/calasparra

Buses – the corner of Calle Teniente Flomesta.

Taxis – rank next to Iglesia de la Merced.

Train station – 4 km out to the north of town.

Buying Property in Murcia

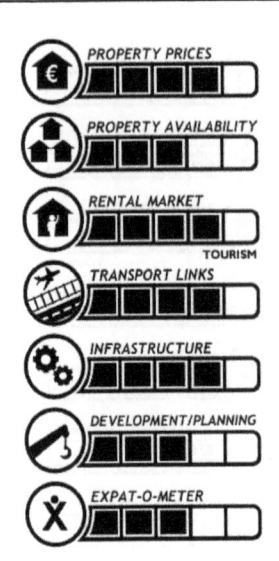

PROPERTY PRICES ▪▪▪▪☐
PROPERTY AVAILABILITY ▪▪▪☐☐
RENTAL MARKET ▪▪▪☐☐
TOURISM / TRANSPORT LINKS ▪▪▪☐☐
INFRASTRUCTURE ▪▪▪☐☐
DEVELOPMENT/PLANNING ▪▪▪☐☐
EXPAT-O-METER ▪▪▪☐☐

Narrow streets and alleys lead towards the castle, which was built in the 15th century and commissioned by the Knights Templar.

Tourist Office - Calle Monjas, 17
☎ 968 702424
www.caravaca.org - click on the link which says callejero for a map.

Ayuntamiento - Plaza Del Arco
☎ 968 702000

Buses - station on Carretera de Granada. Hourly buses to Murcia take 1 hour and 30 minutes and daily buses also run to Lorca.

Taxis - ranks on Calle Incomienda and at the corner of Gran Vía and Juan Carlos I

Caravaca De La Cruz
Population: 23,000

Caravaca de la Cruz is a beautiful medieval (12th and 13th century) town, with many historic, traditional properties in the old quarter. The town has been declared by the Vatican as one of the world's Holy Cities, along with Rome, Jerusalem, Santiago de Compostela and Santa Toribio de Liebana, thus giving Spain three out of five. Caravaca de la Cruz is also allowed to celebrate the Perpetual Jubilee once every seven years. The next time will be in 2010.

Properties range from tiny 1 bed, 1 bathroom (and nothing much else) reforms in the heart of the historic old town for a little less than €40,000 to fincas for between €70,000 and €200,000. There is also the new development, Nature, which will have 4000 homes by 2009 with prices ranging from €200,000+ for a villa or €140,000 for a townhouse.

Parking is a nightmare - so park whereever you can find a space and walk! Once out and about, you'll quickly find a number of museums, such as Museo Sacro de la Vera Cruz (religious artefacts), Museo de los Festejos and also Museo Arqueológico.

Down in the centre of town the main attractions are the Iglesia del Salvador, the monastery at Iglesia de San José and Ermita de San Sebastián (with interesting murals). Around the area you can find the spring at Fuentes de Marqués and various archeological sites at Cueva Negra, Palacia de

Armas, Los Villares, Cerro de la Ermitas and Cuevo del Rey Moro.

Up the hill, you'll find the most photographed church in the area, El Santuario de Vera Cruz, with a pink marble facade. A popular part of the May fiesta is los Caballos del Vino (wine horses), in commemoration of a tradition that took place in the 13th century. The Christians besieged in the fortress by the Arabs managed to break the siege and search for water. When they failed to find any water, they returned to the fortress with the wineskins on their horses filled with wine. The commemoration consists of horses galloping up the steep slopes to the Castle.

At the beginning of May Caravaca has very famous and popular fiestas – Santísima y Vera Cruz meaning good potential short-term rental income.

Cehegín

Population: 14,500

Going due west of Murcia, just before you reach Caravaca and Moratalla, you'll reach the hilltop town of Cehegín.

There are two fiestas in Cehegín (apart form the usual Easter celebrations) the first being the Muestra de Comercio de Artesanía which is at the end of August. And in September the main town fiesta of La Virgen de Las Maravillas is between the 8th and 14th.

Cehegín has lots of properties for sale from huge fincas at just under €1 million right down to tiny townhouses at around €30,000. The townhouse reformation market here is booming.

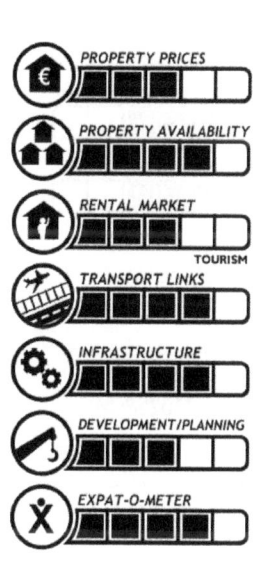

Buying Property in Murcia

Turismo - Calle Begastri, 5
☎ 968 723550

Ayuntamiento Calle Lopez Chicheri, 5
☎ 968 740400
www.cehegin.com

PROPERTY PRICES ■■■□
PROPERTY AVAILABILITY ■■■■
RENTAL MARKET ■■■□
TOURISM / TRANSPORT LINKS ■■□□
INFRASTRUCTURE ■■■□
DEVELOPMENT/PLANNING ■■■□
EXPAT-O-METER ■■■□

Tourist Office
www.moratalla-turismo.com

Ayuntamiento - Calle de la Constitución
☎ 968 730258

Bus Station - ctra de Caravaca - daily buses to Caravaca.
☎ 968 292211

Taxis
☎ 968 730653 / 968 730430

Moratalla has a thriving rural tourism business and I own a townhouse here too if you're looking for somewhere to stay!
www.moratallatownhouses.com

As with several of its neighbours, Cehegín is a medieval town comprising narrow streets and sand coloured buildings. The town is crowned by the Ermita Purísima Concepción, a 16th century creation. From here you get good views of the town and out towards the valley of the river Argos.

Moratalla

Population: 9,000

Moratalla is an old town of Arab origin with narrow streets, rambling up a steep hillside, off to the northwest of the province. The town is capped by a castle with excellent views to the surrounding countryside and forest. It makes a good base for walking and cycling.

Properties range from large country fincas with 250 hectares of mountainside for a little under €1 million to off-plan villas at Balcon de Moratalla for around €300,000 right down to tiny townhouses ripe for renovation from €50,000 and ruins (will need to be knocked down and rebuilt) for less than €30,000.

In the centre of town on Calle Constitución there's a 16th - 18th century convent, Convento de San Francisco, with an exhibit room.

The fiesta for Moratalla is between the 11th and 17th of July for Cristo del Rayo and it gets very busy - meaning good rental prospects during this holiday.

Why Wait Until You're Older?

If you are thinking of putting your Spain plans on hold until after you retire then you could be missing out on the best years of your life in your dream location...

At just 28 and 30 years old respectively, Great Yarmouth couple Julie and Joe now live their dream life in Murcia and are effectively free from the large monthly mortgage repayments that plagued them in the UK.

Now, before you jump the gun, they haven't inherited a penny, they don't have rich relatives, their joint annual income was less than £25,000 and they didn't have to sell their home in the UK.

Joe recalls, "When we decided to buy our place in Moratalla – a four storey townhouse – we actually had credit card debt of almost £3,000 and no savings! So the only way we could raise the deposit for our Spanish purchase was to borrow some more. We shopped around until we got a deal and borrowed £10,000. We knew £7,000 would be plenty as a deposit on the houses we were looking at in Spain, so we consolidated the credit card debt at the same time."

Although borrowing more money when you're already in debt could be seen as a bad idea Joe figured that investing that money into something that was growing in value above the interest rate he had been charged to borrow it made sense. The only problem was that you aren't supposed to use loans as a deposit to buy property.

On raising the finance Joe admits, "Banks are happy for you to get into more debt and buy junk that devalues over time such as cars and holidays but they frown on you using their money to better your financial situation. To me this is immoral so we didn't tell them the whole truth! I told them the loan was for 'debt consolidation and home improvements'. We did use some of the money for debt consolidation and when you think about it – owning 2 homes compared to 1 *is* a 'home improvement!'"

Also, despite now owning 2 homes, both with a mortgage, their monthly outgoings have shrunk from almost £1,000 to just over £500. Joe puts it down to seeing the whole thing as a game.

He explains, "Compared to Moratalla, UK house prices are sky-high. We played to the strengths of this difference by deciding to rent our UK home out and moving to Spain sooner than we had originally planned. Our mortgage repayments at the time were £550 a month and we achieved £625 a month in rental. That effectively transformed a £550 bill into a £125 income overnight and added just one more reason to live in Spain."

He continues, "Because our Moratalla townhouse was so cheap, our monthly mortgage payments, despite it being slightly larger than our UK home, are just under £200. So, taking into account our £125 income, which is slightly less after tax, we only have a monthly mortgage bill for both properties of roughly £75 compared to the £750 it would have been!"

Essentially, Julie and Joe have gone from owning 1 house with a mortgage bill that ate up almost a quarter of their monthly income to owning 2 houses with a mortgage bill that is less than a full tank of fuel. With certain long-term capital growth in both properties and Joe's business, which allows him to work anywhere with an internet connection, their future in Murcia looks secure.

Joe's Tips:

- There is always a way to make things happen if you know what you want – banks like lending you money – so all you need to do is spend it wisely when you get it.

- Even if circumstances mean you probably won't live in Spain until you retire, the sooner you buy your place the better off you'll be as it grows in value.

- If you're serious about buying property then stop buying stuff that devalues. Flash cars might impress some people but they lose value – buy a cheap car and use the cash you might have otherwise spent on a car loan as a deposit or to handle the repayments.

- If you're young and you really want to live in Spain then it helps to find a way of replacing your job income with something you can do from home. See *www.publishingbusinessinabox.com* for details on what I do.

Mula

Population: 14,600

Mula is on the river Mula, and is another hillside town topped with a castle (like Moratalla). Mula is the epicentre for a geological faultline, and has experienced a number of minor earthquakes – in 1999, 2002 and most recently in 2005 so make sure you get good buildings insurance!

Mula is another of those towns found in this part of Murcia where you have an old town with a booming property market. There are townhouses available from as little as €35,000 that will require quite a lot of work. You can also find reformed townhouses for just €40,000. At the other end of the scale, for €1 million, you can have a luxury villa with land and a pool.

Then there's the Trampolin Hills Golf resort where you can buy an off-plan apartment for around €100,000 or a 3-bed penthouse for €200,000.

Castillo de los Vélez (the castle on top of the hill) is 16th century and can be reached by footpaths, which meander up from the top of town.

Local fiestas between the 19th and 25th of September (el Niño de Mula) and also the 15th May for the fiesta of San Isidoro. The Easter celebrations are particularly vibrant in Mula due to the drumming!

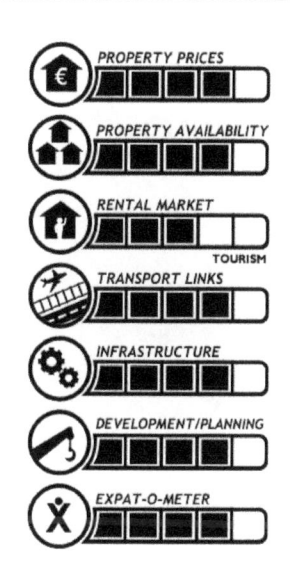

PROPERTY PRICES
PROPERTY AVAILABILITY
RENTAL MARKET
TOURISM
TRANSPORT LINKS
INFRASTRUCTURE
DEVELOPMENT/PLANNING
EXPAT-O-METER

Many of the streets appear to be pedestrianised and you'll be surprised to find a car in the most unlikely of places!

Tourist Office - Calle Doña Elvira
☏ 968 661501

www.mulavirtual.net (good street map and an A-Z - click on "Callejero")

Ayuntamiento - Plaza Del Ayuntamiento
☏ 968 660444

Buses – station on Senda de la Moreira has buses to Murcia and Caravaca

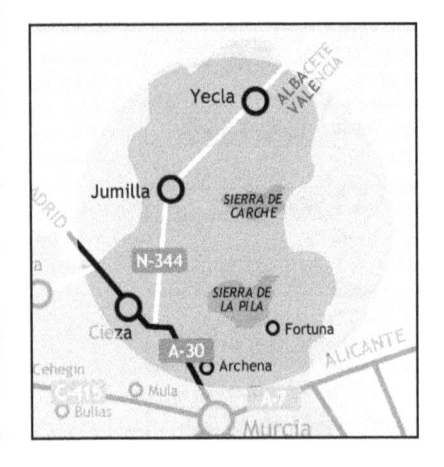

THE NORTH EAST

Overview

A mainly rural area with good motorway access that is due to improve. There are small communities and villages on hilltops. The countryside around these villages is dotted with fincas, grape growing farms and some new builds. There are few urbanisations, though the number is increasing.

PROPERTY PRICES

There are a few new developments and prices are low.

PROPERTY AVAILABILITY

There are a few reforms available in the old towns and some fincas in the campo with just a few urbanizations.

RENTAL MARKET

The Sierra del Carche is a wonderful area of natural beauty. For outdoor enthusiasts there is plenty on offer. It is mainly a rural tourist rental market.

TRANSPORT LINKS

Motorway access is reasonable and due to get better over the next 5 years. Less than 1 hour from the nearest airport. Yecla's proximity to the Alicante province means it is relatively close to Alicante airport.

INFRASTRUCTURE

The towns are well established and cater adequately to their current requirements.

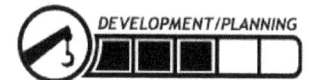

DEVELOPMENT/PLANNING

There doesn't appear to be much going on in the way of new developments, with just a few smaller urbanizations being built.

EXPAT-O-METER

Jumilla has a fledgling expat community.

Developments in the North East

Another recent newcomer to the urbanisation phenomenon, the North East of Murcia has held on to its traditional Spanish feel although there are a few developments of note including:

Residencial Balneario in Campos del Río from Grupo Nicolas Mateos *www.gruponicolasmateos.com*

El Castillo Golf on the outskirts of Jumilla will have 1,400 detached and semi-detached villas, bungalows and apartments built around a 9-hole golf course.

Fortuna Hill Golf will have off-plan apartments, townhouses and villas around a golf course and there's also El Reloj near Fortuna.

There's Casa Don Juan Golf Resort in Blanca from the developers Grupo Prasa and CIMNSA.

A Balneario is a place where you can relax and be treated by thermal and/or mineral waters. People come to the baths in Murcia from all over the world for their curative properties, excellent for tourism.

If you own or know of a development that isn't mentioned here please go to *www.NativeSpain.com* and add it for inclusion in the next edition.

El Jardin del Royo is near Abanilla just north of Murcia city.

Finally Santa Ana del Monte Jumilla Golf resort had stopped issuing bank guarantees to some new clients at the beginning of October 2007. It looks like it is a temporary problem due to overwhelm at the townhall but check first; you should never buy an off-plan without a bank guarantee. When completed it will have a 5 star hotel, shops, bars and a golf course, of course!

Archena

Population: 15,000

Archena can be found on the last natural part of the Río Segura, before it heads into the city (Murcia). Archena is used as a base for visiting the Balneario de Archena and also for walks and excursions up the Valle De Ricote.

There are relatively few properties available here and of those you can expect mainly fincas at around the €150,000 to €400,000 mark.

Balneario Archena is based about 2km from the centre of Archena, where there are a number of hotels and pleasant walks along the Rio de Segura. The thermal baths at Balneario have therapeutic properties, with temperatures around 50° centigrade.

PROPERTY PRICES
PROPERTY AVAILABILITY
RENTAL MARKET
TOURISM
TRANSPORT LINKS
INFRASTRUCTURE
DEVELOPMENT/PLANNING
EXPAT-O-METER

☎ 902 366 902
www.balnearioarchena.com

Ayuntamiento on Calle Major
☎ 968 670 000

Buses - Avenida del Carril with services to and from Murcia

Taxis - rank in Plaza Primero de Mayo

Fortuna

Population: 6,300

The town is dominated by the spa (Balneario), Roman ruins, the crypt reached through a 200m tunnel at Manantial Church, a small palace (Palacio Atalaya) and casino. It's also just 2km from the centre of the Black Caves (Cueva Negra).

There are plenty of opportunities to buy around this area but, due to Fortuna's proximity to Murcia city and its new golf courses, prices here are relatively high. In the resale market you can get fincas for €600,000 or 100 year old townhouses for €50,000. There are also a number of new urbanisations including El Reloj and Fortuna Hills Golf Resort with properties from around €300,000.

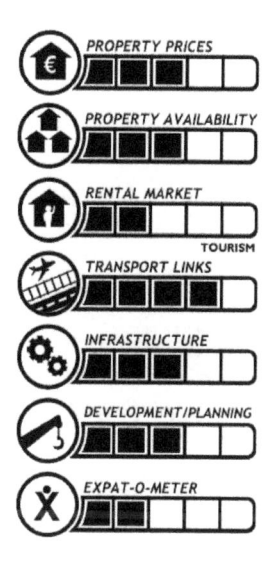

Ayuntamiento - Calle Purísima
☎ 968 685103

Jumilla

Population: 22,200

Far off in the northeast of the region, as you approach Jumilla you will find the endless acres of vineyards hard to miss! The famous wine of Jumilla DOC is the town's main source of prosperity. Overlooking Jumilla is the 15th century castle, which is best seen from the west of the town.

The new Santa Ana del Monte golf resort offers villas for around the €400,000 and apartments at less than €100,000. There are a few ruins in the main town for €50,000+ and there's also the El Castillo Golf resort with prices between €130,000 and €260,000.

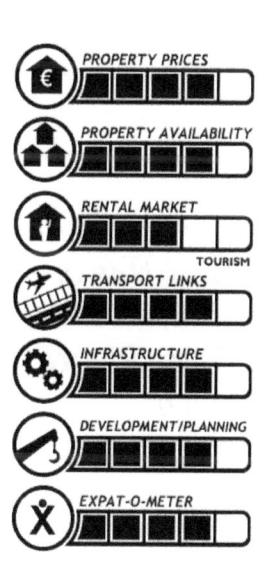

Tourist Office - Avda. de Levante, 13
☎ 968 757682 or 968 716060

Ayuntamiento - Calle Canovas Del Castillo, 35
☎ 968 780112
www.jumilla.org

Buses - Avda. de la Libertad
Taxis - Plaza de la Glorieta

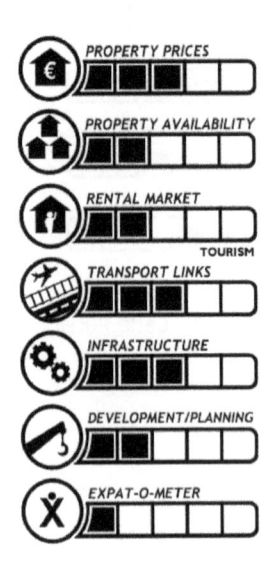

PROPERTY PRICES
PROPERTY AVAILABILITY
RENTAL MARKET
TOURISM
TRANSPORT LINKS
INFRASTRUCTURE
DEVELOPMENT/PLANNING
EXPAT-O-METER

The main towns and villages of this area include: Villanueva, Ulea, Ojós, Ricote and Blanca.

Wine tourism is also strong in the area and there are many Bodegas and wine shops. Jumilla is the primary wine-growing region of the whole of Murcia and perhaps the best-known exported wine from the region. Red and rosé wines are particular favourites.

Ricote Valley

The Ricote Valley, which stretches along the fertile plains of the river Segura, was the last stronghold of the Moors in Spain, and is one of the most beautiful and undiscovered parts of Murcia. The Ricote Valley clings to its Arab heritage, as shown by the numerous remains from this period, including the ingenious rural irrigation system.

There's not much for sale around these parts except on the Casa Don Juan Golf Resort in Blanca which offers properties for around €200,000. Other property consists of €300,000 fincas in Ricote and €65,000 townhouses in Blanca.

Ricote maintains a rich and highly individual gastronomic tradition in which the local wine features strongly! After indulging in the delights of the local cuisine, you may feel like enjoying a few days of healthy relaxation and pampering at the wonderful 19th century spa in Archena very close by.

Sporting activities such as river-rafting on the River Segura, mountain biking or horse riding along routes offered by various riding centres are the most popular activities.

Jumilla Quad!

I'm Sue McGinlay from South London. We've bought a house in Santa Ana del Monte, near Jumilla.

We were looking for a typical working Spanish town with markets, shops, bars and restaurants that didn't just serve British breakfasts and Sunday roasts. We found that in Jumilla plus beautiful scenery, lots of history, excellent wine and very friendly local people.

We had decided that we would prefer to live inland away from the obvious tourist spots. Although we have enjoyed holidays in Galicia and the Basque country the climate there is too much like the UK! We came on a couple of viewing trips in this location before deciding that we liked the area enough to want to live here and we spent a week in the local town of Jumilla before deciding to pay the reservation fee.

Santa Ana del Monte is a golf resort on the outskirts of the wine town of Jumilla. We have bought a quad (two semi-detached houses backing onto another two semis). We have met many of our new neighbours and they are moving for similar reasons to us and so we have made many new friends already. Also, about half of the purchasers are Spanish which we see as a very positive sign.

We'll leave behind rain, the stress of working in London (especially the commuting), the cost of eating out and living generally - oh, did I mention the rain? Of course we are both leaving our families behind too, however they are queuing up to spend their holidays with us!

I work part-time as an administrator and also work as a complementary therapist. John works as a civilian for the Metropolitan Police.

We both hope to work part-time when we move to Spain and I hope to improve my Spanish to the extent that I can give complementary therapy treatments to local people. We would also like to work with businesses in the local town of Jumilla and arrange holidays with a difference: not just running in the beautiful countryside around Santa Ana del Monte, but wine tastings at local bodegas and walks along Jumilla's historic trail.

If you go to the local tourist office you can get a map of the town which shows the historic trail and it is well worth spending a day exploring it. Don't miss the Botanical Gardens on the outskirts of the town either. We enjoyed a 10 euro menu del dia at the Casa Molowny which is on the edge of Jumilla on the road to Hellin. It was very popular with the locals too, which is always a good sign!

It is very important to speak as much Spanish as you are able to, as people really appreciate you making the effort. In Jumilla many people don't speak English - and why should they?

I advise everyone to make sure that you do your research first and even when you think you have found the ideal location spend some time there before deciding to buy. If there are two of you then both of you should give the properties you view marks out of 10 to ensure you are equally keen, as this is a major, life-changing decision!

Sometimes I think people might be unrealistic in their expectations: expecting the lively summer holiday resort to be as lively during the winter months and expecting to find work when they don't speak Spanish.

If I had to choose just one thing that I love about my new home it would be the mountain views. But I also love the town of Jumilla, which is just up the road, the friendliness of the local people plus, of course, the wine!

The only things we miss from home are our friends and families, but nothing else. We can always visit them if we run out of Marmite! We have no regrets so far. Hopefully I will give the same answer if you ask me in 10 years' time!

Yecla

Population: 30,900

The northernmost town of Murcia is Yecla (96 km north of Murcia).

Don't expect many bargains around here. Fincas typically start from €1.3 million and country houses fetch €150,000.

Up on the hill you'll find the Santuario de la Purísima Concepcion, which offers great views of the town and surrounding areas. There is also a castle, Castillo de Yecla, from the 14th century. There are many churches in the town and the old town is quite beautiful but rather short on bars, restaurants and cafes.

The principal industry of Yecla, besides wine, is the manufacture of furniture with 40 furniture shops along one road alone!

The fiesta of San Isidro is in the middle of May and their Fiesta Patronales is in December.

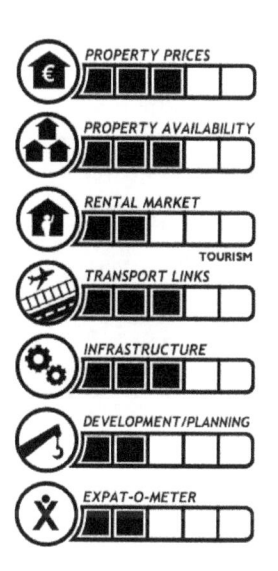

- PROPERTY PRICES
- PROPERTY AVAILABILITY
- RENTAL MARKET
- TRANSPORT LINKS / TOURISM
- INFRASTRUCTURE
- DEVELOPMENT/PLANNING
- EXPAT-O-METER

Yecla is one of the three wine producing areas with its own DOC in Murcia (the other two being Bullas and Jumilla). The name Yecla comes from the Arab word Yakka.

Tourist office
☎ 958 754104

Ayuntamiento – Plaza Mayor
☎ 968 751135 or 968 718000
www.ayuntamientoyecla.com

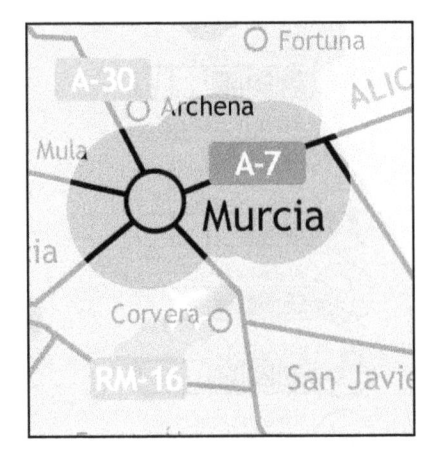

MURCIA
Overview

Murcia is well established with beautiful apartments in the old quarter while the suburbs are a mixture of urban sprawl and smallholdings.

The city and surrounding suburbs are in constant flux at the moment. Cranes can be seen in all directions as new apartments are being built all around the city. Although the old part of the city is protected from high-rise, to the north there are some taller buildings sprouting up.

PROPERTY PRICES

Prices are good for the location considering the abundance of infrastructure and facilities.

PROPERTY AVAILABILITY

There are lots of second hand modern properties available all around the city. There are new apartment blocks being built.

RENTAL MARKET

Mostly longer term rental opportunites. Very little in the way of tourist rentals. There are theatres, cinemas, museums and excellent nightlife so this may change.

TRANSPORT LINKS

Excellent motorway access. Between 45 mins and 1 hour from the nearest airports.

INFRASTRUCTURE

As can be expected from a well-established city all necessary infrastructure is in place. Roads are well maintained, transport infrastructure is improving (AVE train to Madrid is planned) and health and social services are adequate.

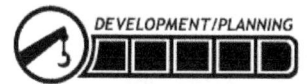

DEVELOPMENT/PLANNING

More developments are springing up. Lots of brownfield sites are being repurposed. Many large out of town shopping malls with new purpose built blocks.

EXPAT-O-METER

Few expats choose to live in and around the city. This is mostly for Spanish.

Developments in Murcia

In and around the city there are lots of developments that coincide with the ongoing commercial developments in the area. Recent new shopping malls - including Ikea - a new football stadium and further redevelopment of brown field sites all point to good growth potential for people buying in and around the capital.

The main strategies of the government include:

- creating new types of social housing which respond to citizens' demands
- promoting renting as a means of access to adequate housing
- sustainable development of land

"Active housing policies are comprehensive. We are working towards achieving the access of all citizens to adequate housing in a socially cohesive city, which is more economically viable and which respects the environment."

www.mviv.es

Buying Property in Murcia

- promoting conservation of existing housing
- rehabilitating neighbourhoods.

There is a huge, well-established development called Altorreal to the northwest of the city near Molina de Segura, which has one of the oldest (1994) golf courses in the region.

The developer MetroVacesa (*www.metrovacesa.com*) has a number of sites around the city, including: Edificio Montblanc (apartments in the expansion zone of the city) and others in Lorca and the Mar Menor.

Also from MetroVacesa is Balcones del Thader, next to one of the new shopping malls (Parque Comercial Thader), which offers high-rise flats and apartments.

Puerta de Murcia is a development of 71 properties again near the new commercial and urbanisation zones to the north of the city. The developer is Lar Crea ☎902146646

In the Plan Parcial Nueva Condomina there's Las Torres de Nueva Condomina. The developer is ALIANZA ☎968899900. Alianza also has Terrazas Green in the same development zone.

Finally there's Monasterio de los Jerónimos near the Catholic University and Frondoso Valley and Torre Guil near Sangonera La Verde.

If you own or know of a development that isn't mentioned here please go to www.NativeSpain.com and add it for inclusion in the next edition.

Iglesia Catedral de Santa María en Murcia – commonly called Murcia Cathedral – there are 25 bells from the 17th and 18th centuries all individually named

Murcia City
Population: 370,800

The city of Murcia is set in the heart of a rich fertile plain at just 43 metres above sea level. Unlike the rest of the region, where the terrain is dry and rugged, the soil here is irrigated by the River Segura and the land has been widely and fruitfully cultivated.

In the city itself the old quarter is made up of a maze of narrow streets huddled together around the Cathedral. This labyrinth is only broken by the main roads crossing through it such as the Gran Vía Escultor Salzillo.

The most pleasant parts of the city, indeed the most typically Murcian, are to be found around the gardens on the banks of the River Segura. A considerable chunk of the population of Murcia does not in fact live in the city itself but rather in houses and farmsteads scattered around it.

A wide variety of fruits and vegetables are grown not only for the Spanish domestic market but also for export to the rest of Europe. For this reason Murcia is often referred to as La Huerta de Europa: The Market Garden of Europe.

In the suburbs you can find duplexes for just under €100,000 and flats from €80,000. Flats in the much sought-after centre of the city go for as much as €1 million.

Murcia Cathedral was built between the 14th and 18th centuries, with some parts being rebuilt in 1735 after flood

Within the city planning procedures ensure that residential and commercial properties are well mixed, with people living above shops, offices being interspersed with homes all within the same apartment block. Parking tends to be underground (though of course double and triple parking on the streets is a national pastime). This leads to a café culture and most areas of the city being populated at all times, day and night.

Tourist Office – the main turismo is at Plaza de Julián Romea, 4 (opposite the theatre) – open weekdays except during the siesta
☎ 902 101070

There is another at Plaza Cardenal Belluga.

There is also a kiosk at Plaza San Francisco
☎ 968 216801
www.murciaciudad.com or www.murciaturistica.es

Ayuntamiento – Glorieta de España, 1
☎ 968 358600
www.ayto-murcia.es

Buses – The main bus station is to the west of centre on Calle Sierra de la Pila, 1
☎ 968 292211

Taxis – are by the train and bus stations and at various other places around the city such as Plaza Martinez Tornel, Avenida de la Libertaz and Calle Alfonso X. You can also call for a taxi on
☎ 968 248800 / 968 297700

Trains – station is at Plaza de la Industria to the south of town
☎ 968 252154

damage. You can get great views, almost 100 metres up, in the tower which dates from the 18th century, when it's open (which isn't often).

Across from the Cathedral is a striking modern building which is part of the Ayuntamiento complex and, surprisingly, complements the Baroque cathedral facing it across the square at Plaza Cardenal Belluga. This building was designed by Rafael Moneo.

The Jardin Floridablanca is a great place to escape the heat of summer under the shade of its well-established rubber trees. It was established in 1848 by Carlos III and was the first public garden to be built in Spain.

Other points of interest are the Museum of Murcia and the Hydraulic Museum, the water mills of the Segura river in Murcia and the surrounding villages which make up the Region.

Murcia also benefits from a diverse programme of festivities: Carnivals (February), Easter (March/April), the Spring Festivals (March/April), the Fair of Murcia (September), and Christmas (December), which, together with cinema, theatre, music festivals, conferences and art exhibitions mark out the animated cultural life in the city. Many of these events take place in the "Teatro Romea" and "Centro de Congresos" of the Region of Murcia.

Easter is a perfect time to visit Murcia to see a traditional Spanish fiesta – Semana Santa – the ornate wooden sculptures of the city's famous artist, Salzillo, are paraded throughout the city. Just after Semana Santa is the

Spring Festival (*Fiestas de Primavera*) – a week-long party that includes the outstanding Bando de la Hurta and the *Entierro de la Sardina* ('burying of the sardine').

Hospital – The region's main hospital is to the southwest of the city off the Murcia to Caravaca highway, called Arixicaca, between el Palmar and Alcantarilla.

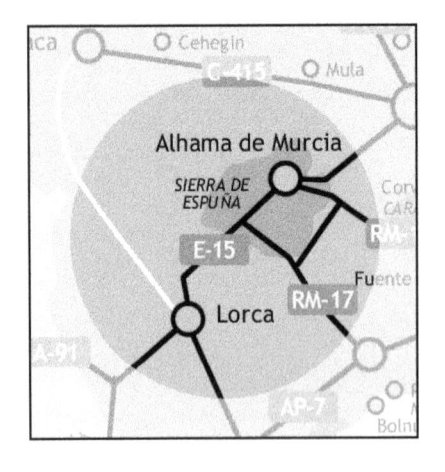

THE SOUTH WEST

Overview

With four relatively large towns in this area it is bustling and busy. The centre of the towns retain their typically Spanish aspects although the sprawl of buildings around them is very modern. There are lots of new urbanisations and the new motorway further opens up access to this developing area.

PROPERTY PRICES

Prices have been going up recently in all sectors.

PROPERTY AVAILABILITY

There are some reforms available in the old towns, though the prices are higher than further north. Also some fincas. There are lots of new developments.

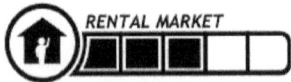

RENTAL MARKET

With the Sierras to the north and a 30-minute drive to the sea this is a great location for tourist rentals. Another excellent area for outdoor interests.

Mostly holiday rentals, this area appeals to rural tourists. Access to the beaches is easier than from the more northerly regions, providing a wider tourist range.

TRANSPORT LINKS

Good motorway access, due to get better over the next 5 years. Between 1 and 2 hours from the nearest airport.

INFRASTRUCTURE

All of the large towns have adequate facilities and infrastructure.

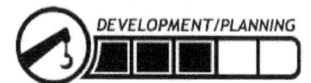

DEVELOPMENT/PLANNING

More developments are springing up. This area has some of the larger new developments.

EXPAT-O-METER

Due to the urbanisations there are large enclaves of expats. The main towns also have small expat communities.

Developments in The South West

The new motorway access around this region has fuelled a variety of large new developments and has also improved access times to the Coast.

Sol, Mar y Natura (Sun, Sea and Nature) between Totana and Aledo is one new development and Mirador Del Castillo in Lorca, which is mostly apartments, is due to complete at the end of 2007. The developer is MetroVacesa (*www.metrovacesa.com*)

A large Polaris World development is also in progress in the Alhama de Murcia area where there are 19,000 flats and villas. It is split into zones, including: Condado de Alhama, Cortijos de Alhama, El Mirador de Alhama & Jardines de Alhama. Find out more at *www.polaris-world.es*

Lorca Resort Golf & Spa in the Sierra de la Almenara nature reserve will have 1800 homes, from the developer Grupo ALZE. *www.grupoalze.com*

If you own or know of a development that isn't mentioned here please go to *www.NativeSpain.com* and add it for inclusion in the next edition.

With just 95 properties, Residencial Espuña is only 5 minutes drive from the town of Totana.

Monte Aledo Resort is made up of apartments, villas and semi-detached properties. The development will have a glass dome (like a Centreparcs) www.inverconinternational.com

Alhama De Murcia

Population: 16,400

Alhama is a city with fruit in the valleys and pines on the mountains lying at the foothills of the Sierra Espuña.

This town boasts some of the most expensive new golf resort urbanisations in the area with villas at more than €1.5 million and apartments from €100,000. You can also find the odd renovated cavehouse for €160,000, studios on the golf complex for €85,000 and shared ownerships for around €50,000. There are also some houses in the town itself but they are harder to find.

In Plaza Vieja at the end of Calle Larga there are some 19th century stately houses with brightly coloured facades and the old town hall, which houses the museum. You can go up to the Arab castle using side streets off Calle Vergara. In the same area you will find the baroque Iglesia de san Lázaro.

Also nearby you'll find the famous bathhouses of the town.

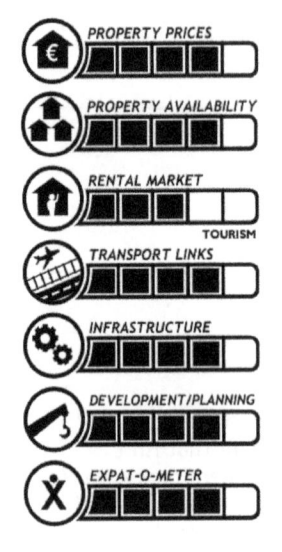

Tourist Office - Plaza de La Constitución
☎ 968 633512

Ayuntamiento
www.paralelo40.org/alhama

Trains - served by both the Aguilas - Murcia line and also the Lorca - Barcelona line.

Lorca & Puerto Lumbreras

Population: 77,500

Lorca is a genteel city just off the main Águilas – Murcia motorway and forms another portal to the Sierra Espuña. The town's most interesting architecture is from the 16th century onwards.

There's a lot for sale in this area including huge fincas from €500,000, village houses from €60,000, plots of land and lots of villas and apartments on the new urbanisations.

The castle in Lorca, which can be seen from a great distance, started out as an Islamic fortress between the 8th and 13th centuries and the oldest parts of the castle, the essential water systems, still remain. Today the castle is used for many town activities including fiestas and civic functions.

Possibly the most outstanding church in Lorca is La Colegiata de San Patricio, which was built between the 16th and 18th centuries and towers over the central part of town. The Iglesia de San Mateo which was built principally in the 18th and 19th century has a stunning vaulted interior.

Lorca's Easter celebrations are probably the most splendid in Murcia (depending upon whom you talk to!) The local fiesta is on 8th September for la Virgen de Las Huertas.

Continuing west from Lorca you reach the town of Puerto Lumbreras, the final town in Murcia. Not too much to say about this town, except it's the furthest point west in Murcia and from here you can see the white washed

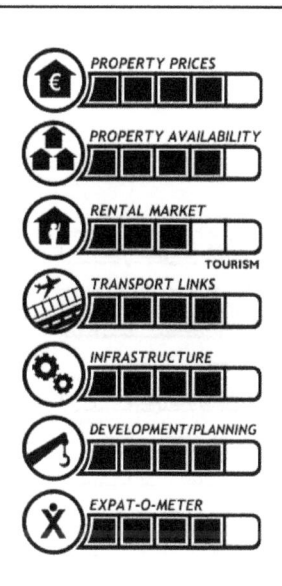

Tourist Office - Calle Lope Guisbert, 12
☎ 968 466157
www.ajuntalorca.es

Ayuntamiento - Plaza De España
☎ 968 407000

Trains - on the Murcia - Águilas line - station on the outskirts of town towards the motorway junction.

Buses - station next to the train station, not only to Murcia but also Granada

Taxis - ranks at Plaza de Calderón, Plaza Ortega Melgares, Calle Glorieta de San Vicente and Plaza Óvalo.

Buying Property in Murcia

villages of neighbouring Andalucia.

There are fincas for around €300,000, apartments for a little over €100,000, some townhouses and quite a few land plots for sale.

PROPERTY PRICES
PROPERTY AVAILABILITY
RENTAL MARKET
TRANSPORT LINKS — TOURISM
INFRASTRUCTURE
DEVELOPMENT/PLANNING
EXPAT-O-METER

Sierra Espuña

The Sierra Espuña is a Parque Regional, which is right in the centre of the Murcia region between the rivers Pliego and Guadalentín. It is actually an artificially planted forestry project which was started in 1891 to combat the deforestation which resutled in erosion and flash floods.

The park contains some of the higher peaks in Murcia, including the Espuña mountain (1585m), Pedro López (1566m) and Morrón Chico (1446m).

There are a couple of information centres in the park itself: Puerta Espuña and Las Alquerras.

It's usual to get to the park by car, from Alhama or Totana in the South West of the region, (the more adventurous can walk or go by bike from these towns).

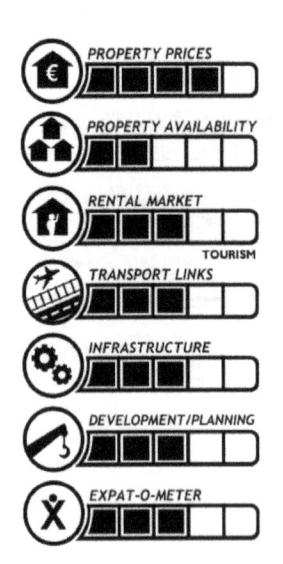

In 1995 17,804 hectares were declared Parque Regional, giving it a protected status. This is an area of outstanding natural beauty and a tourist attraction.
www.sierraespuna.com

Walking and cycling in the vast park area is becoming increasingly popular making towns in the vicinity ideal locations to buy holiday lets for the growing adventure tourism market.

There are a variety of walks and cycle routes through the park that are best described in the book Descrubrir Sierra Espuña from Natursport
☎ 609 623061
www.natursport.com

Locally there is also the town of Pliego, lying on one of the transhumance routes, used until recently to move livestock from summer to winter pastures.

When We Hit Our "Wants" List

We are Susie Bearder and Steve Hill originally from Hampshire, UK. We now live in Rambla de Nogalte, Puerto Lumbreras. We moved with our parents in 2006 and have no regrets whatsoever.

About five years ago we became very dissatisfied with our situation in the UK. It was a combination of factors. I (Susie) had to give up an interesting and well-paid job after becoming disabled by illness. Our financial situation had become critical. Steve's mother was widowed but had lived in Spain for many years and did not wish to return to the UK. Incremental changes or discontents just kept piling up but one of the most shocking incidents was when I fell in the high street of my village and three cars drove by without helping. Eye contact was made so these people have no excuse really...

Also UK food had become an issue because of the nature of my illness, multiple sclerosis. Diet is a critical factor in staying well and the Spanish diet is very healthy - as long as you watch your alcohol consumption that is!

To come here Steve gave up his job, an enormous thing for him to do. Family and friends on the whole were fairly scattered around the south of England and both of my children are grown up with their own busy lives but both were constants.

We have a new build rustic style house with an old casa, which still remains next door which we use at present for storage. As of today we have finally gone on the national grid - a day of celebration!

Our neighbours are a bit wild, occasionally noisy but we don't see much of them – like foxes, badgers, wild boar, snakes. We still don't have an address except for the one on the ayuntamiento computer in Lorca. We do have a human neighbour the other side of the mountain. She's very nice and we are very likeminded we think.

The best things about living here are the beauty and tranquillity. People seem to think we are isolated but we think that is a state of mind. I felt more isolated in the English village we left behind. This area is covered with special places and we keep finding more by the attitude "what happens if we take this road?" The history of the area will keep us busy for yonks as will the great little eating places one discovers if prepared to leave the beaten track or follow the Spanish lead. Mind you we have introduced our Spanish friends to the odd place as well.

Buying Property in Murcia

For the time being this is definitely our home. We still have much we would like to do here and there is still that every day/every year stuff that we have to get on with like our second year picking almonds, preparing land etc.

We have five acres of land to care for with almonds and olives. I'm a photographer and Steve has to be the physically fit one who keeps us all on the straight and narrow with two over pensionista age. We may take on other things yet but we still have plenty to do without looking for any more. Our menagerie does, however, keep increasing. I take photographs, blog, paint, write and sell books at a local market once a month.

Doing your homework is incredibly important and much can be done through the Internet. We had looked all over Valencia, Alicante and north Murcian regions. We made several offers but in the end we backed out knowing that something was not quite right usually on the advice of our lawyer.

I was using *www.propertynet.com* on a daily basis to look at new properties and that is where this house popped up. We found the estate agents very friendly, helpful and professional with a good website so we could send info back to Steve. Steve made meticulous lists about what he wanted to know.

Of course things are never perfect and I have discovered ways to sound off through my writing, which I do through the *www.nativespain.com* forum and through my interest in the natural world and association with the Iberianature forum.

Susie's Tips:

- Remember to work out what the weather is like all year round.
- Have an independent lawyer well versed in property law.
- Know what is on your wants list.
- Not learning the language, or at least attempting to learn some, is one of the mistakes people make when they come here. How would it feel if the boot was on the other foot? It is vital to be able to speak Spanish if you wish to have a full participating life in Spain and not just an English speaking enclave.
- We only miss Marmite and English movies on a big screen. But having just returned home after our first visit we realise there is nothing terribly important that we can't get through living here.
- The internet helps enormously - add a webcam and you are away.

Totana

Population: 24,700

One of the principal attractions of Totana is just outside town towards the Sierra Espuña. The Santuario de la Santa is nestled in a valley to the northwest of town, this 17th century monastery decadent in striking pink stands out against the green of the pine forest.

There are lots of fincas available for around €300,000, a few townhouses at €150,000 (reformed) and €80,000 (in need of renovating), some plots of land and villas on the new urbanisation for around €280,000.

The area is also known for pottery and there are a couple of shops in the centre specialising in selling local pieces with a number of other workshops out of town between the N340 and the road to Mazarrón.

The local fiesta in Totana is on 7th January each year.

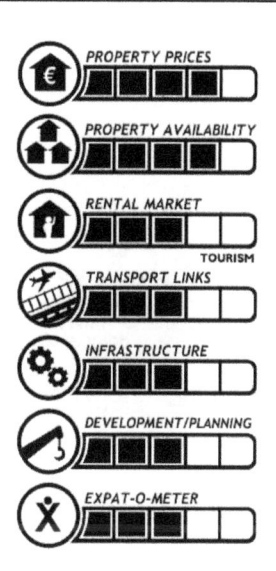

PROPERTY PRICES
PROPERTY AVAILABILITY
RENTAL MARKET
TOURISM
TRANSPORT LINKS
INFRASTRUCTURE
DEVELOPMENT/PLANNING
EXPAT-O-METER

Tourist Office - Avenida del General Aznar, 12
☎ 968 423902
www.ayto-totana.net,
www.totana.org or
www.totana.com

Ayuntamiento - Plaza De La Constitucion, 1
☎ 968 418151

Buses - station on Calle Juan Carlos I - with buses to Murcia, Mazarrón and Lorca

Trains - station out to the southeast of town - served by Águilas - Murcia line.

ÁGUILAS & MAZARRON

Overview

Águilas is a bustling seaside town, with strong Spanish roots while Mazarrón and the port are very popular with tourists. There are lots of unspoilt beaches along this stretch of the coast with the main developments staying very close to the towns. Being a popular tomato growing area, massive plastic greenhouses can be seen stretching right down to the waterfront in places.

PROPERTY PRICES

Very few bargains to be found.

PROPERTY AVAILABILITY

Second hand properties exchange hands frequently. Some new urbanisations with off-plans.

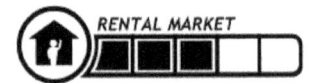

RENTAL MARKET

With the beaches, mountains and towns it's an excellent area to live or visit. There is also the nature reserve of Cabo Cope, great for walkers, bird-watchers and scuba divers.

Mostly holiday rentals, this area appeals to Brits, French, Germans and Dutch. The holiday rental period is long. There is high competition though as there is oversupply of rental accommodation.

TRANSPORT LINKS

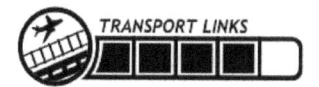

Excellent motorway access, due to get better over the next 5 years. Between 1 and 2 hours from the nearest airport. Buses run frequently during the summer months.

INFRASTRUCTURE

The infrastructure and amenities here are generally well-developed.

DEVELOPMENT/PLANNING

Though there are very few high-rise buildings along this part of the coast planning permission has in the past been quite lax. There is very little room for new developments, though of course there are a few.

EXPAT-O-METER

There are many expats (British and German mostly) in this region. 5,000 Brits live permanently on the Camposol urbanization.

Developments in Águilas & Mazarron

Thankfully, the coastline around here is well protected and there are few big developments. Those larger developments tend to be a little inland just a few kilometres from the beach.

The developments of Residential Callados Golf, Villa Marina Seaside Resort, Jardines de Cope, Golf Los Terreros and Mundo Aguilon, Los Collados Resort, Playas de Calabardina are all in Águilas.

There's also Mazarron Country Club and Camposol (with multiple "sectors" and new off-plan builds). Camposol is one of the most established urbanisations in the area from Grupo Masa (*www.grupomasa.com*) is inland a little way from the coast near Mazarron.

In the port (Puerto de Mazarron) there's El Alamillo and other small gated communities and a little further towards the east is El Pinar de San Gines in La Azohia and Mojon Hills in Isla Plana.

If you own or know of a development that isn't mentioned here please go to *www.NativeSpain.com* and add it for inclusion in the next edition.

Águilas

Population: 28,000

This southwestern city near the Murcian coast has an arid and mountainous landscape, extensive beaches with crystalline cliffs and small, little frequented coves.

There are villas for €500,000, luxury apartments from €350,000 (many within walking distance to the beach) and lots of new developments with prices ranging between €150,000 and €300,000. There are also a few townhouses for sale for renovation from around €120,000.

The hill where the 18th century Castle of San Juan of the Águilas is based was a refuge to a population afraid of pirate attacks. Its dilapidated condition prevents access to the interior, but it offers an excellent vista of the town and the surrounding coast.

The Port, which is dominated by the lighthouse, leads to the wholesale fish market, where at 5pm there's a daily fish auction.

Many tourists come to see the natural splendour of the region and, if you travel on from the beach at Poniente, you'll reach a group of coves - Cuatro Calas. These are in a protected area, so are not only great places for quiet sunbathing, but also good for walks.

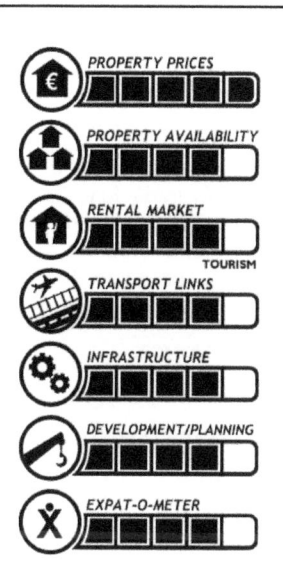

PROPERTY PRICES
PROPERTY AVAILABILITY
RENTAL MARKET
TRANSPORT LINKS / TOURISM
INFRASTRUCTURE
DEVELOPMENT/PLANNING
EXPAT-O-METER

In February Águilas enjoys Carnaval, which has a Rio de Janeiro feel about it, with 3 days and nights of floats, processions and fancy dress.

Tourist Office - Plaza Antonio Cortijos
☎ 968 493285
www.aguilas.org
www.aguilas.tv

Ayuntamiento
☎ 968 418800
www.ayuntamientodeaguilas.org

Taxi - ranks can be found on Calles Isaac Peral and Munoz Calero

Buses - stop at the bar on the corner of Avenida Juan Carlos I and Calle Carlos Marín Menú with services to Almería, Cartagena, Lorca and Murcia.

Trains - run 3 times a day to Murcia and Lorca.

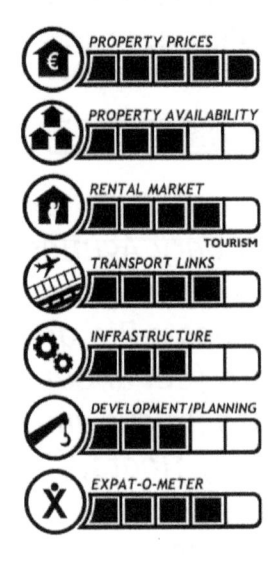

PROPERTY PRICES
PROPERTY AVAILABILITY
RENTAL MARKET
TOURISM
TRANSPORT LINKS
INFRASTRUCTURE
DEVELOPMENT/PLANNING
EXPAT-O-METER

Tranquil beaches with fine sand, huge cliffs and beautiful coves can be found at nearby San Pedro, Blanca and Los Hierros. Los Hierros is dominated by the tower named Torre De Cope, which has been attacked on numerous occasions by pirates. Close by are the beach at Calabardina and the natural park of Calnegre-Cabo Cope.

Bolnuevo

Population: 260

An upmarket seaside resort near Puerto Mazarrón, Bolnuevo has one of the most recognisable landmarks of Murcia – the weathered sandstone formation that adorns most of the region's brochures and tourist guides.

Property prices start at around €150,000 in this area with villas for about €500,000.

Following the coast road to the southwest brings you to miles of beautiful, and often secluded, coves and beaches including a number of nudist spots. The road is very narrow and pitted so keep your wits about you as it's mostly only wide enough for one car.

Carrying on further towards Águilas you reach Punta Calnegre where there are more organised family-friendly beaches. These are best reached by car from the Mazarrón - Águilas road.

Mazarrón

Population: 20,900

A functional market town that has sprung up out of the old mining industry in the area. The region used to mine the mountain ranges which were rich in lead, zinc, silver, iron and alum. The remnants of the mining industry can be seen throughout the region.

There are quite a few established urbanisations in this area with prices ranging, for a small villa, from just over €120,000 to €400,000 for the more upmarket properties. There are some small urbanisations and walled-in private properties set around swimming pools. There is a lot for sale around here so take your time to look around.

Mazarrón is the central shopping area for a number of satellite housing estates, such as Camposol and there are many useful DIY (bricolage) shops just out of town towards Puerto Mazarrón and the outskirts.

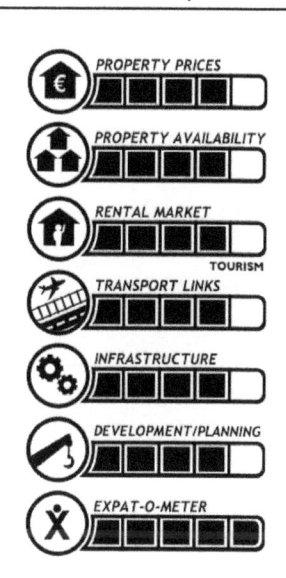

PROPERTY PRICES
PROPERTY AVAILABILITY
RENTAL MARKET
TRANSPORT LINKS TOURISM
INFRASTRUCTURE
DEVELOPMENT/PLANNING
EXPAT-O-METER

Tourist Office - Avenida Doctor Meca, 47
☎ 968 594426

Ayuntamiento - Plaza de Ayuntamiento
☎ 968 590119
www.mazarron.es

Taxi - ranks on Calle Juan Paredes and Plaza del Muelle

Buses - station on Avenida Doctor Meca with 3 buses a day to nearby Cartagena.

Buying Property in Murcia

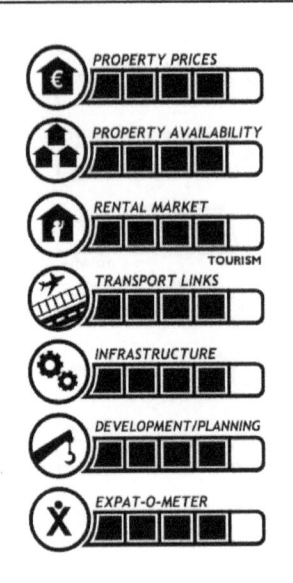

PROPERTY PRICES
PROPERTY AVAILABILITY
RENTAL MARKET
TOURISM
TRANSPORT LINKS
INFRASTRUCTURE
DEVELOPMENT/PLANNING
EXPAT-O-METER

Tourist Office - Calle Doctor Meca, 20
☎ 968 594426

Puerto Mazarrón

Population: 5,000

Not to be confused with Mazarrón this seaside town is the centre of much of tourism on the south coast and Mediterranean.

There are literally hundreds of properties for sale in this area strecthing along the coast. Many of the available properties are resale properties on existing small developments, with a few new developments thrown into the mix for good measure. Prices are relatively high, as you'd expect near the coast, with frontline beach apartments costing between €200,000 and €500,000. Villas can be bought for around €250,000 and some apartments in the town for as little as €100,000.

There are good beaches – in fact 35km of them – as you head northeast out of town and all along the coast towards Aquilas. Follow the road east to reach the many seaside towns including La Azohia.

CARTAGENA AND THE CAMPO DE CARTAGENA

Overview

There are a number of towns that fall within the area of Cartagena and the whole valley is referred to as Campo de Cartagena, which is a huge plain running some 50 km north-south and 50km east-west. Some of the towns are covered below. This inland area is also known as The Golf Valley due to the number of new developments springing up here.

There are also numerous small towns and villages all around Cartagena and along the coast from El Portús to Portman.

PROPERTY PRICES

Prices have risen for rural and townhouses. Prices for property on urbanizations and new developments have slowed, though many still increased in the last year.

PROPERTY AVAILABILITY

Due to the massive expansion in this area there are many properties for sale.

RENTAL MARKET

With the Mar Menor and the Med within 30 minutes access, beach and sea activities are easy to access. There are plenty of exisiting golf courses and more being built. Within the urbanisations there are often good entertainment opportunities, usually catering to an expat market.

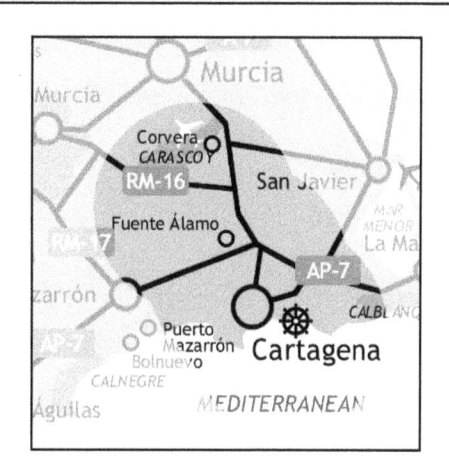

Mostly holiday rentals. There is oversupply. Some of the off-plan developments offer guaranteed rental income (take care and consult a solicitor).

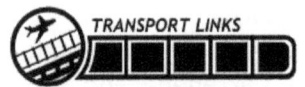

TRANSPORT LINKS

Good motorway access which is due to get better over the next 5 years. Just minutes to the airport, plus there is due to be a new airport built by 2010.

INFRASTRUCTURE

The amenities and infrastructure are growing daily. The road network has been improved. Many of the urbanizations are planning their own hospitals and schools.

DEVELOPMENT/PLANNING

Many developments are planned and underway. This area is classed as the golf valley, for good reason. All along the C3319 you will see cranes and new developments springing up.

EXPAT-O-METER

Many expat communities and growing. This is where Brits come to play golf.

Developments in the Campo De Cartagena

Known as The Golf Valley, unsurprisingly, this is where the main developments have sprung up in the last 7 or so years. Since a new motorway (C3319) really opened this area up many new developments followed all along its 30km length. The majority of these new developments have a golf course attached.

A total of four developments from Polaris World (*www.polarisworld.com*) are located here. La Torre Golf Resort with a "town centre" arranged around the lake has everything from supermarkets to a hotel and spa. There's El Valle, with a golf course, hotel, restaurants, bars and pubs all planned to be on site.

Built around a late 19th century, colonial-style country house, near Sucina, Hacienda Riquelme, with approximately 1,800 apartments and a central golf course will include the usual restaurants, bars and shops on site. Finally you have Mar Menor Golf Resort comprising 750 properties a 5-star hotel and the usual restaurants and bars.

Mosa Trajectum Golf from Key Resorts, ☎902734717, is still undergoing development and will have shops, bars, restaurants and a medical centre.

The resort of Valle del Sol is just off the C3319 between Murcia and San Javier airport and there's also Los Granados Golf Resort in Gea y Truyols.

3 Molinos Resort, from CA Mediterraneo Hispa Group SA, is another new resort with two golf courses, a sports and equestrian centre, theatre and art gallery all in the planning stages.

La Loma, with only 470 properties, is one of the lowest density new urbanisations in the area and includes a golf course.

If you own or know of a development that isn't mentioned here please go to *www.NativeSpain.com* and add it for inclusion in the next edition.

Trampolin Hills Golf Resort from Grupo Trampolin (*www.grupotrampolin.com*) is on the C3319.

United Golf Resort Bamendi will have around 5,000 properties. There's also La Tercia Real from the same developer, which should be complete some time in 2008 and will include a golf course.

Paraleja Golf is expected to have the first phase open in the summer of 2008 with full completion by 2012.

Sierra Golf Balsicas, in Balsicas, from Grupo Masa has all types of property for sale.

Sucina Golf and Country Club is scheduled for completion in 2008 and will include the usual restaurants, golf and leisure facilities.

On the other side of the Murcia-Cartagena A-30 motorway you also have Corvera Golf & Country Club, in the Carrascoy mountains, which is a large development of apartments and villas from the developer Calidona – *www.calidona.com*.

There's also Hacienda del Álamo near Fuente Álamo (*www.hdagolf.com*), which already has one golf course and another one planned. By the end of 2008 they also aim to have a "town" with equestrian centre, tennis, restaurants, banks and a 5-star hotel.

Destiny, Debating and a Dog...

I'm Martine Cherry from Codsall, South Staffs, UK. I currently live in El Carmoli, Cartagena, Murcia. I moved here in 2004 with my husband Bill.

If you believe in fate then our move to Spain does have the feel of destiny or if you are more pragmatic, like my husband, it is the fruit of discontent, many hours of long debate (often with red wine included) and hours of research and planning.

When we first viewed Spanish property we were shown nothing we felt we wanted for a holiday home, let alone something that would make us consider a permanent move. 'By chance' a parental friend mentioned he owned a property on Costa Cálida. "Where?" was our response. Feeling we had nothing to lose we took an afternoon off and went in search of a town called Los Alcázares.

The old fashioned, almost charmingly shabby look and feel of the place delighted us and the incredibly tranquil Mar Menor very quickly won us over. We found a townhouse which met all our requirements and as we explored the area more we realised we had struck gold. Indeed we had many holidays, short breaks and even our honeymoon in that house.

As we were spending more and more time in Spain we got a good insight into local business and our own career experience helped us spot a potential opportunity of our own. We began working in the property market on a very small scale and found we really enjoyed providing people with a truly professional way to find a property in such a lovely area.

While our Spanish business was in its infancy we still worked in the UK embroiled in corporate life. However the more time we spent in Spain on business the more we recognised that our UK careers were not providing us with enough satisfaction in return for the rounds of endless meetings, conference calls and long distance journeys.

Our main source of satisfaction was coming from applying our experience to help people within our Spanish venture. We were at our happiest sitting in our supermarket bar listening to the locals chat or discovering new places in the region.

We talked about living in Spain endlessly but it seemed like it would and could only be talk. Our next Spanish property purchase was an unplanned but unanimous decision made completely with our hearts.

We were chatting with a colleague who mentioned houses had been released that very day with fantastic views of the Mar Menor in a quiet Spanish village. Ten minutes later we had arrived at the site, plans in hand. In that moment we could already feel the sea breeze on the terrace, see our long walks on the beach and taste the tapas at the local bar. Our heads soon dosed us with reality when we had to work out if we could actually buy the house and ask our solicitor to check if it was legally sound which, to our relief, it was and we could!

At first we still saw this solely as a second home but we had the final push towards our move when the company we worked for started voluntarily downsizing; finally presenting us with the opportunity to leave and run our business full time.

It was a difficult decision involving lots of business planning, number crunching and soul-searching as we knew moving to Spain was the only option if we wanted to expand the business properly.

Yes it felt daunting but also completely right.

We left behind two teenage step-daughters, parents, sisters and brother, nephews, nieces, friends, a great little real ale pub and two well paid corporate jobs.

Since then we have, of course, had our ups and downs. But we've never had so many happy and memorable days. We've gone shopping for Christmas sprouts and come back with a dog, seen an eighty year old man fly a loop in the sky and watched our clients fall in love with this part of Spain, just as we have. It's not one thing that makes us love living here, it really is a big cooking pot filled with local characters, family culture, great activities, history, scenery, sunshine, great food and drink and a completely sane but, at the same time, crazy attitude to life.

I still maintain it was pure good fortune in finding our place in the sun! Like many people back then we had never heard of Murcia or the Costa Cálida but relied on the recommendation of one man – we are indebted to him!

We live in a three bedroom, semi-detached house, on the side of a hill with a big terrace which looks out across the Mar Menor. The area is residential, mainly Spanish and there are lots of Spanish second homes here. In the summer the area is alive with the sound of holiday makers and fun. There is a little open air cinema we can see from our balcony and we have a friendly local bar run by an extremely hardworking Spanish family – Antonio, Adila and their boys. Our immediate neighbours are English but most of the community are Spanish and are very friendly and warm.

The best thing about living here is the feeling of light, space and tranquillity.

We run an independent property agency – helping people find the right property in the area, assisting them with the buying and after-sales process. For new build properties one of the key steps is identifying reputable builders who build quality properties in the right location and sell them at realistic prices. We work hard to develop good relationships here so that we can offer our clients the best properties in the area and when there is flexibility, arrange payment schedules to meet their circumstances.

When a property is under construction we send out progress photographs and when the property is completed we can help the clients with setting up the property – furnishing, lighting etc.

We work within our local area to identify excellent re-sale properties and we offer straightforward, candid advice about valuations and marketing. If needed we help our clients find an independent solicitor and can guide them through the process of setting up a Spanish bank account – essential in Spain.

We provide our clients with no-pressure, no-obligation viewing visits – designed by themselves for themselves. Our website *www.dreamspain.net* is our shop window and we regularly update prices and availability so that clients get an honest view of property prices in the area. We also include photographs and details of this lovely area, so that prospective clients can get a taste of what they will see if they visit us.

Our long term plan is to continue our business, helping clients find the best property in the area and introducing them to the treasures of the region. We want to continue to enjoy our business and leisure time, improving our knowledge and use of Spanish and developing our network of friends and business associates in Spain.

There are obvious mistakes people make when thinking about moving abroad, like not researching the area etc. but recently I've seen more people discontented because they have moved out as a couple or family and not everyone has been behind the decision, or one partner has moved purely to satisfy the other. It can be a recipe for disaster if not everyone finds their own purpose and sense of satisfaction here.

I recommend that you always have a back-up plan. Even with the best planning, intention and luck things may not turn out the way you dream. Always think "what if?" and have a fall-back if things don't work out or circumstances change. If you are moving out as a couple or family then really understand each other's aspirations and needs - it can be stressful and you need to have a shared goal to work towards.

It takes time to recognise and accept differences in culture and attitude here, especially in the business world, but it is part of adjusting to a new way of life.

I think it is important to be able to speak Spanish - not to necessarily become fluent but to be able to get by day-to-day, deal with emergencies and be courteous in public etc. Of course the ideal is to become fluent but it takes lots of time and hard work - not a 7 day miracle CD!

We sometimes miss our family and friends but they visit often so we don't have to miss them for very long. We missed curries at first but we've now got a great little Indian supermarket and Bill has learnt how to cook a whole variety of tasty curries.

I sometimes regret that we didn't make the move earlier but in reality the timing in our lives would not have been right.

Cartagena City

Population: 185,000

Situated in the southeast of the region is Murcia's second city - Cartagena - which is a maritime town and port with a history stretching back to Roman times. The main road is Paseo de Alfonso XIII, to the south of which lie most areas of interest, including the city's port (pedestrianised area) and tourist sites.

There are modern flats in the city from €150,000, luxury apartments at around €500,000 and new build apartments from €120,000.

The majority of tourist attractions have a maritime theme, perhaps the most obvious example being the submarine from 1888, which is installed at the port end of the main pedestrianised shopping area.

There is a naval museum, an under water archaeology museum and (although not open to the public) a large arsenal up on the hill overlooking the city. Near the bullring there's a recently re-discovered Roman amphitheatre which is currently undergoing renovation.

If you have a car you'll be able to drive to many fortresses, castles, fortifications and battlements, ranging from Roman construction through to abandoned 20th century projects. Cartagena's military importance is charted by numerous installations including huge guns on the hilltops, submarine tunnels straight out of a James Bond film set and 16th century pirate look out towers.

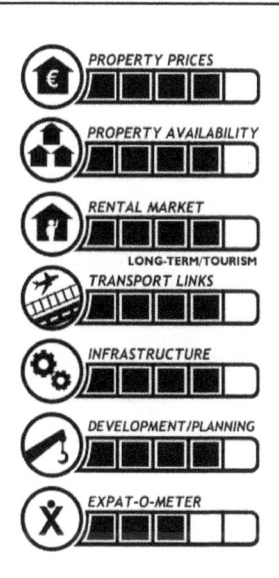

PROPERTY PRICES
PROPERTY AVAILABILITY
RENTAL MARKET LONG-TERM/TOURISM
TRANSPORT LINKS
INFRASTRUCTURE
DEVELOPMENT/PLANNING
EXPAT-O-METER

International nautical week in June and the Mar de Músicas festival in July are two of the most popular fiestas.
www.lamardemusicas.org

Tourist Office - Plaza de Bastarreche
☎ 968 506483
www.ayto-cartagena.es

Ayuntamiento - Calle Sor FCA. Armendariz, 6
☎ 968 128800
www.cartagena.es

Trains - the station at Plaza de México has trains running to Murcia and on Plaza de Bastarreche local trains go to Los Nietos on the Mar Menor.

Buses - station on Calle Trovero Marín

Taxis
☎ 968 311323 / 968 531313
968 558038 / 968 311515

Fuente Álamo

Population: 10,000

Going into Fuente Álamo is rather like visiting Croydon. Shut your eyes and listen to the plethora of English accents. We wouldn't like to mislead you into believing that Fuente Álamo is a worthwhile tourist destination, however it does serve a number of useful purposes - including an excellent selection of banks, a Post Office (where you can hire a post office box - Apartado de Correo) and a passable selection of DIY shops.

Fuente Álamo also has a new golf complex (Hacienda del Álamo) to the northwest which attracts even more Brits. Prices here range from €800,000 for a 4-bed villa with swimming pool to €175,000 for a small apartment. There are also some fincas around starting at around €150,000 and some townhouses at similar prices.

Their fiesta, San Agustín, runs from August 18th to 28th when the town resembles a sprawling fun fair.

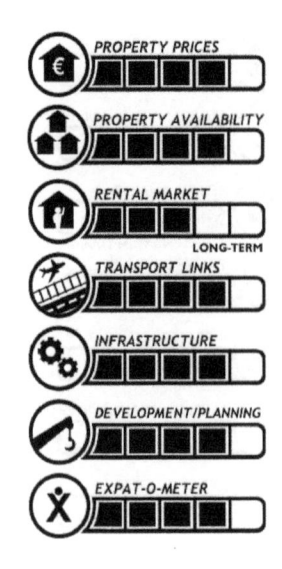

Ayuntamiento - Plaza Constitucion, 1
☎ 968 597001 / 968 597585
www.ayto-fuentealamo.es

THE MAR MENOR

Overview

The Mar Menor consists of a large number of smaller towns mostly along a stretch of coast. The properties here are mainly for holiday rental and used during the summer months extensively and some of the towns become very quiet outside of the tourist season. You will find plenty of Spanish tourists here alongside the Brits, French and Germans.

PROPERTY PRICES

Prices are high, especially for the more well-known and established developments.

PROPERTY AVAILABILITY

The area is still undergoing development, though not as much as in the past.

RENTAL MARKET

With the beaches and the golf courses, recreation is assured. Many of the town have bars and restaurants that cater to the expat market, including menus in multiple languages and entertainment designed for expats.

Mostly holiday rentals. There is some oversupply including lots of new hotels being built on the golf courses.

TRANSPORT LINKS

Excellent motorway access. Very close to the nearest airport.

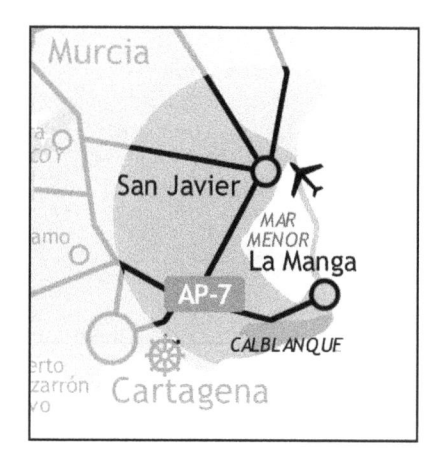

Buying Property in Murcia

INFRASTRUCTURE

Good infrastructure, well-developed area.

DEVELOPMENT/PLANNING

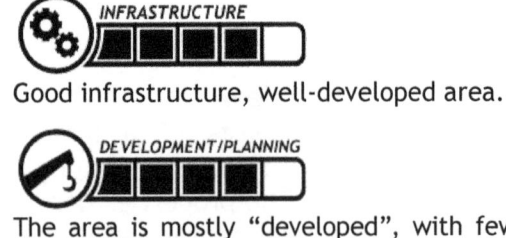

The area is mostly "developed", with few opportunities for new developments. Those that are new are well thought out and in-keeping with the current properties.

EXPAT-O-METER

Plenty of expats in this part of Murcia, though there's still a good sprinkling of real Spain too. English is spoken in many of the bars and restaurants.

Developments in the Mar Menor

There are many urbanisations around the Mar Menor that have been established for a few years so there are plenty of re-sale properties available. However, due to the development rules around the coast, there are fewer new builds in as there just isn't that much space left.

The best-known development in the area is La Manga Club and the Las Lomas Village in Los Belones, where there are the famous golf courses, luxury hotels and excellent facilities in a very well established, attractive and well-maintained location.

In Los Alcazares there is Isla Marina, Molino de la Pueblo which is due for completion at the end of 2009 and Golf Torre del Rame to the south (from MetroVacesa – *www.metrovacesa.com*) which is due to be completed at the end of 2008.

If you own or know of a development that isn't mentioned here please go to *www.NativeSpain.com* and add it for inclusion in the next edition.

Rocio Beach, Aldea Sol II and Pinada del Mar Menor can all be found in Santiago de la Ribera.

Roda Golf and Beach Resort, just outside San Javier, from Calidona (www.calidona.com) opened in 2006 and a new hotel is opening in 2008.

Lo Romero Golf Course, on the border between Murcia and Alicante province, was due to open in 2006 but is still under construction.

Work on Novo Carthago from Hansa Urbana (www.novocarthago.com), which consists of apartments, townhouses and villas, began in 2007 and will have 2 golf courses.

Cabo de Palos is a marina town with a famous lighthouse up on the hill. Although it's a heaving, trendy place in the summer, tourists still visit off-season to enjoy the food.

Cabo de Palos
Population: 550

Across from the Marchamalo salt flats, Cabo de Palos is a small point of land jutting out into the Mediterranean. Naturally equipped with many small bays and inlets it has always been a centre for fishing. The main port area here is one of the prettiest on the entire coast. Using fresh local fish and vegetables, some of the best restaurants in the area line the traditional quayside and offer very reasonable prices.

You can buy a penthouse overlooking the sea for €170,000, a 3-bed apartment for €400,000 or a modern townhouse for €250,000.

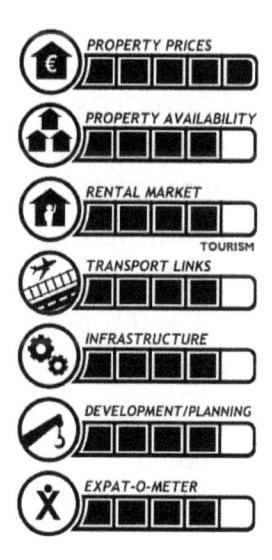

PROPERTY PRICES
PROPERTY AVAILABILITY
RENTAL MARKET
TOURISM
TRANSPORT LINKS
INFRASTRUCTURE
DEVELOPMENT/PLANNING
EXPAT-O-METER

Buying Property in Murcia

PROPERTY PRICES ▰▰▰▰▰
PROPERTY AVAILABILITY ▰▰▰▰
RENTAL MARKET ▰▰▰▰▰
TOURISM
TRANSPORT LINKS ▰▰▰
INFRASTRUCTURE ▰▰▰
DEVELOPMENT/PLANNING ▰▰▰▰▰
EXPAT-O-METER ▰▰▰▰

La Manga

Most Brits who know anything about this region will have heard about La Manga ("the sleeve"), due to its enormous golf course, the "housing estate" of the same name and the infamy of British footballers. However La Manga Club is somewhat a misnomer as it's actually south of the true La Manga. However for simplicity we'll include both in this description.

The true La Manga is the geographical feature that separates the Mar Menor from the Mediterranean. This heavily developed strip, which is some 21km long and in places only 100m wide, can be seen from many kilometres inland. La Manga has a number of pleasant beaches and is, in places, home to the jet set with a few stunning marinas.

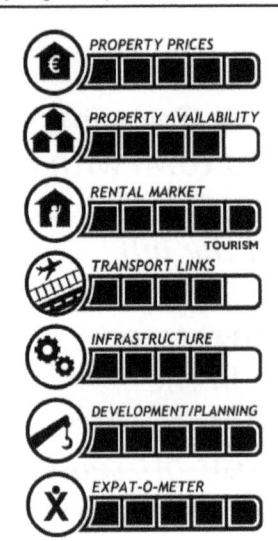

The hotels along La Manga are popular with Spaniards and this really was the first area of tourist development in the region. It's now popular with Brits and Germans too.

There are lots of places for sale around the area so there is plenty of choice for all budgets. You can get a studio apartment for under €100,000, an apartment with garage for around €300,000 or a villa for €1 million.

If you're looking for something in La Manga Club itself then you can get a 5-bed villa for €1.6 million or a penthouse apartment for €500,000.

La Manga can only be reached by car from the south (Cartagena end) and the spine of La Manga is a busy service road providing access to the hundreds of hotels and holiday flats here.

Tourist Office
☏ 968 146136

Great website with excellent up to date information on the La Manga complex and surroundings:
www.lamangawind.com

Lo Pagán

Population: 1,500

Lo Pagán is a seaside town at the northernmost cusp of the Mar Menor, with therapeutic mud baths and a long sandy beach, with calm waters. The appeal of this area (coupled with San Pedro del Pinatar) revolves around the salt marshes, which is now a protected Nature Park. Migrating birds use the marshes as a stop-over and bird-watching is popular. The mineral content of the mud makes it a sought-after remedy or conditioner, especially for the skin, and there are several therapy spas nearby.

You will find mostly apartments and townhouses here with prices from €180,000 to €280,000.

On the seafront there is a commercial fish market in the Parque del Mar Juán Carlos I. Nearby is the regional park of las Salinas, which is home to a variety of protected birds and wildlife. On the salt flats you will see flamingoes and herons in particular, and if you're very lucky a flock will fly overhead while you're bathing on the long sandy beaches.

Lo Pagán is the easternmost town on the Murcian coast sitting on the tip of the Mar Menor.

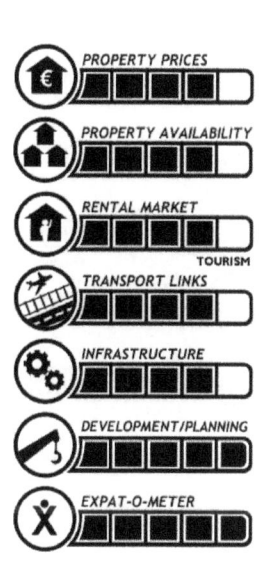

PROPERTY PRICES
PROPERTY AVAILABILITY
RENTAL MARKET
TOURISM
TRANSPORT LINKS
INFRASTRUCTURE
DEVELOPMENT/PLANNING
EXPAT-O-METER

The towns and beaches themselves combine to form the most popular Mar Menor resort offering a wide variety of bars, restaurants and a good little marina.

Buying Property in Murcia

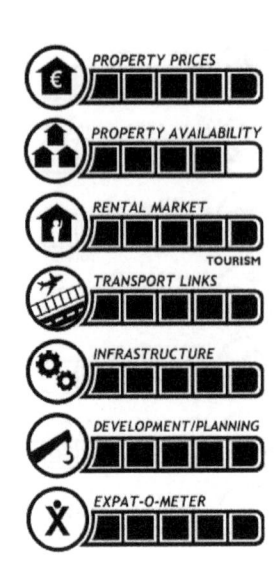

PROPERTY PRICES: ▮▮▮▮▯
PROPERTY AVAILABILITY: ▮▮▮▮▯
RENTAL MARKET: ▮▮▮▮▮
TOURISM / TRANSPORT LINKS: ▮▮▮▮▯
INFRASTRUCTURE: ▮▮▮▮▯
DEVELOPMENT/PLANNING: ▮▮▮▮▯
EXPAT-O-METER: ▮▮▮▮▯

Central on the west side of the Mar Menor the Romans and then later the Arabs used Los Alcázares as an ideal location for thermal baths.

Tourist Office – Calle Fuster, 63
☎ 968 171361
www.losalcazares.com

Los Alcázares
Population: 6,000

There's plenty for sale here, including many small plots of land with water, electricity and fences for around €100,000.

Also, you can get apartments on the urbanisations for around €150,000, small townhouses for €200,000 and villas for a touch over €1 million.

A commercial bike scheme will be introduced (though a date is difficult to ascertain!) with initially 300 machines available for hire at a modest charge. This will fit in perfectly with the plan to build a network of cycle tracks throughout the town. A botanical garden covering 40,000 sq metres will also be constructed (due date is also currently unknown) adjacent to Nueva Ribera and the La Hita beach.

Other projects planned for the near future include a new Conference Centre (Palacio de Congresos), Cultural Centre, School of Nautical Activities and Tourist Information Centre.

The newish Balneario Commercial Centre near the Mercadona has over a dozen food outlets including an excellent Thai/Vietnamese/Cantonese (Cocina Asiatica Run) and good Indian (Hindustani Roti Sharaabi Bar). A short distance along the Avenida de la Libertad is the Oasis Centre which has a mixture of more eating establishments including some that cater for the all-day breakfast brigade. For those who are home-sick there is the Big Breakfast Butchers which can provide British cuts, barbecue meats and home-made sausages.

Despite the multitude of developments here Los Alcázares is still very Spanish with a maze of narrow interesting streets. Parking seems to be easy apart from July-August when the Spanish arrive on holiday.

In August (15th to 30th) they have their local fiesta (Semana de la Huerta) when groups representing market garden areas throughout Spain and other European countries gather to display their folklore, handicrafts and prepare gastronomic feasts from their local produce. Fiestas are popular here; there's a week-long fiesta in mid October and a Medieval one at the end of March.

Los Alcázares is still very Spanish with a maze of narrow interesting streets.

Mar Menor

The Mar Menor is the largest salt lagoon in Europe. Its waters are rich in iodine and never get deeper than 7 metres. It has 170 km2 of area (42,000 acres) and 73 km of coast.

This is a closed sea which maintains a warm temperature all year except for December and January when only the most hardy Brits will brave the waters. The Romans and the Arabs built thermal baths around the coast here and, to this day, people visit the area for the therapeutic properties of the bathing.

There are considerable salt works in the area, which coincide with important ecological reserves for

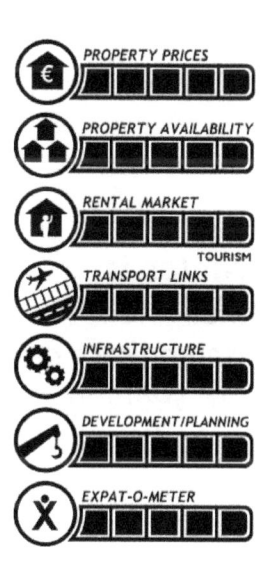

Buying Property in Murcia

birds, plants and other wildlife.

To get a good view of the Mar Menor, take a walk up the hill Cabezo de la Fuente from Los Belones village (near La Manga golf complex)

Some notable buying spots (also see Los Alcázares, San Pedro del Pinatar, Lo Pagán, Santiago de la Ribera) include:

Los Urrutias - A relatively new resort, Los Urrutias has almost a mile of golden beach with good facilities, enhanced by an unusual offshore marina in a hexagonal shape. The coast either side is protected land, preserving the quality of the environment. For €160,000 you can find a small duplex or €500,000 will get you a villa on the La Perla estate. Or on Residential Balcones del Mar Menor (near El Carmoli) you can find villas between €200,000 and €500,000.

Behind the beach at Los Urrutias is a modern, spaciously laid out town with an attractive promenade and public spaces.

Los Nietos - Divided into an 'old town' just off the coast and a newer resort area with a very good beach, Los Nietos is another Mar Menor town with a popular marina. Big enough to have a life all year round, it is popular with buyers seeking a place to live, as well as holidaymakers. Linked to the city of Cartagena by rail, it is especially suitable for those who prefer to travel by public transport. Small townhouses start from at least €200,000, apartments in Villa Cristal begin at €140,000 and beachfront apartments go for €280,000.

Los Nietos is popular with holidaymakers and people seeking a place to live.

Mar de Cristal - Separated from Los Nietos by a small river, Mar de Cristal is a compact and friendly little resort with three good beach areas and a new, pretty promenade with bars and restaurants. A good-sized marina adds to the charm. There are plenty of apartments at the €160,000 mark and duplexes at €300,000+.

Playa Honda & Playa Paraiso - At the very southern end of the Mar Menor, these two beach areas have seen quite a bit of expansion in the last few years and have evolved into fully-fledged resorts. They are nestled along the coast with the hills of the Calablanque Nature Park behind, the protected Marchamalo salt flats to the side and the whole length of the Mar Menor in front. You can get small apartments for €130,000, villas for around €300,000 and luxury villas for €500,000.

These two resorts have seen quite a bit of expansion in the last few years.

Shh... Don't Tell Anyone!

Do you sometimes think that the Region of Murcia is Spain's best-kept secret? Even the Spanish outside the region don't know about it! We discovered Murcia in 2001 when we drove down the La Manga Strip, it was love at first sight. The long golden beaches, palm tree lined roads and warm November sun, we were besotted and like the best love stories we let our head rule our heart and bought a property! We had not planned to buy a property in Spain, we were visiting the area to take photographs for our website.

We are not normally impulsive people, but we do have the motto 'don't just dream it, do it!' if we want to do something and we can afford it then we will do it. Our plan at that time was to buy a larger house in the UK, the mortgage was in place, we realised that we could buy an apartment overlooking the Med for the price of gaining another bedroom in the UK. Within four weeks we had paid the deposit and signed the purchase agreement.

The love affair with Murcia has continued and just keeps getting stronger. Since our first visit, we have visited the region every month and spent hours touring the area, as we sell property in the area it has been a case of mixing business with pleasure. We now specialise in selling property in the Region of Murcia as we feel it has everything to offer the holidaymaker, investor and those wishing to relocate. We are also fascinated with the many undiscovered tourist attractions in the area and until this book was published, very little was written in English.

On our travels we have visited many wonderful restaurants, most of which look like a transport café from the out side, but turn into fabulous traditional Spanish restaurants with impeccably dressed waiters, linen table cloths and sumptuous menus. If you are really adventurous and don't speak Spanish you can always have the 'menu del dia' for 8€ (a three course meal with wine), we have discovered some wonderful dishes, especially the potato and meat stew which is served as a starter. We travel throughout the region and have already made a note of over 40 recommended restaurants, we are developing a tourism website, so that we can share these little gems with other adventurous diners.

The other delights that we have discovered are usually connected with food, such as the restaurant at the bottom of the cliff and over hanging the river at the Santuario de Esparanza, near Calasparra. Who would have expected to find a church built into the rocks? The

Spanish flock here in their hundreds on a Sunday, they also take picnics and Barbeques and meet up in huge family groups to exchange the news (rather noisily) There are so many exciting places, the Sierra Espuna with its fantastic views and you may see the wild boars if you are lucky, the bustling markets that are held in most towns, the wine regions of Jumilla and Bullas, the sacred cross at Caravaca and many more.

They also know how to party and can teach us Brits a thing or two. The magnificent costumes and traditional food and wine at their Fiestas which take place all through the year is another secret which we sometimes stumble on by accident, but once we have found them we make a note in our diary to return next year.

The love story continues and we are constantly finding out more and more, we feel as if we are still on honeymoon with years and years of getting to know the Region of Murcia ahead of us and hopefully there will still be some more surprises ahead!

Gill and John Hughes
www.direct2spain.co.uk ☎0044 1743 364830

Buying Property in Murcia

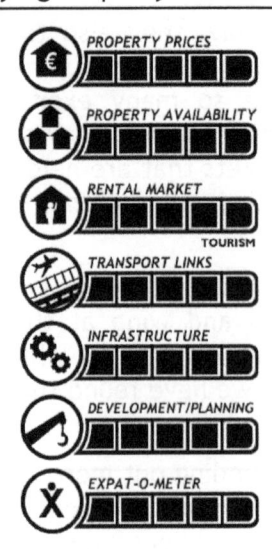

PROPERTY PRICES
PROPERTY AVAILABILITY
RENTAL MARKET
TRANSPORT LINKS — TOURISM
INFRASTRUCTURE
DEVELOPMENT/PLANNING
EXPAT-O-METER

Tourist Office - Calle Padre Juan
☎ 968 571704
www.turismosanjavier.net

Ayuntamiento - Glorieta Garcia Alix
☎ 968 571401

Trains - Balsicas - 10km away.
Buses - Autobus Urbano -
Autocares La Inmaculada
☎ 968 180659 / 968 571401

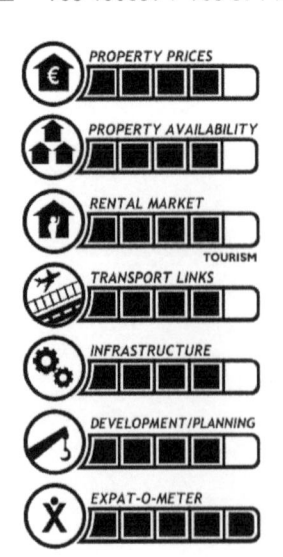

PROPERTY PRICES
PROPERTY AVAILABILITY
RENTAL MARKET
TRANSPORT LINKS — TOURISM
INFRASTRUCTURE
DEVELOPMENT/PLANNING
EXPAT-O-METER

San Javier
Population: 20,200

Just inland from the Mar Menor, its tortuous one way system is probably known to most first time visitors to San Javier airport 3km away!

However, once on foot, tourists will find some 17th century churches including La Ermita and the Iglesia de la Virgen del Rosario. San Javier also has excellent shopping and leisure facilities including an impressive sports centre.

You can get a log cabin ("lodge") here from €115,000 on the 20-plot Lemon Grove development while €150,000 to €200,000 buys you an apartment on an estate and €500,000 should be enough for a villa.

Since 1998 San Javier has been the home of an increasingly popular jazz festival held in late June.

Santiago De La Ribera
Population: 3,500

Perhaps the most attractive of the Mar Menor resorts Santiago de la Ribera sits on the shores of the Mar Menor directly in front of San Javier and the two are closely linked.

Home to a superb marina area and some of the best restaurants in the region it is no surprise that luxury villas and manicured gardens are the standard in Santiago De La Ribera.

This town is very popular with the "townies" from Murcia at the weekends, especially in the summer.

For €120,000 you can get an apartment at Aldea Sol II and €200,000 to €400,000 will buy you a townhouse at Pinada Del Mar Menor.

The promenade at Santiago de la Ribera has been reconstructed and there are two restaurants located side-by-side on the beach. Restaurante Lonja Mar Menor is open for lunch and evening meals all year round. The Pescaderia-Restaurante Miguel is open all day in the high season but lunches only out-of-season. It also has a resident colony of cats (I counted 15) that live under the wooden floorboards and are very friendly if you are eating fish!

San Pedro del Pinatar
Population: 16,700

Just south of Lo Pagán on the Mar Menor you'll find San Pedro del Pinatar. These two towns pretty much run into each other. As well as a few majestic 19th century villas there is also the Museo de Mar in Calle Lorenzo Noral.

€120,000 will buy you an apartment and €350,000 will buy you a villa on Residencial Pueblo la Sal. You can also find the odd townhouse for at least €400,000.

San Pedro's local fiesta (fiesta patronal) is on 29th of June and they have a Flamenco festival in July.

Tourist Office - Calle Padre Juan
☎ 968 571704
www.marmenor.net

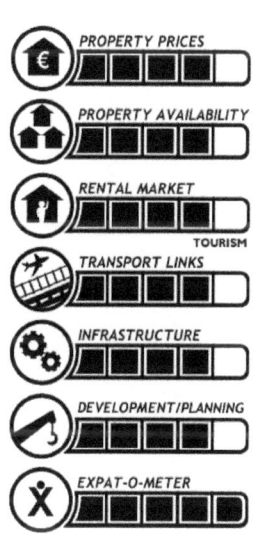

PROPERTY PRICES
PROPERTY AVAILABILITY
RENTAL MARKET
TRANSPORT LINKS / TOURISM
INFRASTRUCTURE
DEVELOPMENT/PLANNING
EXPAT-O-METER

Tourist Office - Parque de los Reyes de España
☎ 968 182301
www.sanpedrodelpinatar.net

Ayuntamiento - Plaza Luis Molina, 1
☎ 968 180661

Buses - station on Alalde José María Tárraga
Taxi - rank on Calle Victor Pradera

BUYING GUIDE

Why Are You Planning to Buy Here?

INVESTMENT

Just three words here – Location, location, location. Murcia really comes up trumps in this regard, with new regional developments (trains, planes, roads etc), superb weather, glorious countryside and unspoilt beaches.

However, the location that suits one kind of investor could be completely inappropriate for another, so it's time to examine your own motives for buying here.

Long Term Capital Growth

Those who are in no immediate rush to make a return on their investment and are looking for longer-term growth (to supplement their pension for example) have the most options as, generally, property anywhere in the region will increase in value over the long term.

If you're buying with a mortgage and expect somebody else to fund the repayments while your asset appreciates, however, then choosing areas with good long-term rental prospects, say cities or large towns, will make your life a lot easier.

It is also worth bearing in mind that ill-chosen locations that are likely to be degraded by developments such as airports, motorways and overbearing urbanisations could end up losing you value that could take a long time to recover.

The location that suits one kind of investor could be completely inappropriate for another.

Short Term Capital Growth

If you are excited by the recent high growth in the Murcia region and see this as a profitable marketplace then bear in mind that you're not alone and the market has slowed somewhat recently.

People making fast-money in the property market here typically fall into 1 of 3 broad groups:

1. **Speculators** – your plan might be to buy offplan (below expected future market value) on new developments and resell the property at a higher price before completion. However, as you are not directly adding any value yourself you have to rely on favourable external conditions that are beyond your control. This could be considered a high-risk strategy and is more suited to those who've done serious research or people who have a gambler's mindset.

2. **Renovators** – the strategy here is simple. Buy run-down properties (at an exceptional discount), renovate them and then sell them at a profit. This is a genuine value-adding approach to property investing as you could be breathing new life into a town's economy as a result. However in the popular old towns, where lots of renovation is going on, local builders can and *will* charge a premium for their services. You also need to check what you can do to a property, especially in the countryside, carefully.

3. **Builders** – this is the ultimate value-add approach and is only really available to those with big pockets. Builders range from those buying land or ruins and creating 1 or 2 homes to giants who swallow up whole chunks of countryside (arguably degrading the area) to build mini-cities and golf courses while providing jobs to the local economy.

Income (holiday and residential lets)

If you want good year-round holiday rental income from property then the first place to look will be along the Costa Cálida and Mar Menor where the mild climate will provide you with tourist business for at least 9 months of the year.

There are many (mainly golf-related) resorts further inland too but these are obviously not going to be as popular as the locations where you can have a golf and beach holiday all in one.

Finally, if you prefer to cater for the more culturally minded tourist, including local Spaniards too, then townhouses, fincas and casas rurales near to the region's many national parks and beauty spots could prove popular. Holiday lets in some towns will be particularly sought after during major religious festivals and fiestas too – but do your homework on how much you're likely to get in rental before you commit.

If you're going for brand new properties or apartments on new resorts then bear in mind, that until

A casa rural is usually a self-catering village house but the term also can also refer to a bed and breakfast or guesthouse. Casas rurales are organised and promoted regionally.

www.noratur.com
www.murciaturistica.es

the resort is complete and mature you may not get many people wanting to take a holiday there.

Of course, if you'd prefer to deal with longer-term tenants then cities and larger towns with a good local working population would make more sense than more touristy spots.

Some figures from 2006 from the government site *www.carm.es* make for interesting analysis.

Number of Apartments for Rent in Murcia (2006)

Cities and larger towns with a good local working population would make more sense if you're looking for long-term rental.

	Apartments	Beds
TOTAL	1,956	8,362
Abanilla	11	32
Águilas	5	28
Alcázares (Los)	227	946
Aledo	8	48
Archena	23	75
Bullas	8	24
Caravaca de la Cruz	22	60
Cartagena	341	1,449
La Manga del Mar Menor	268	1,152
within Cartagena	73	297
Cehegín	10	23
Fortuna	8	40
Lorca	8	35
Mazarrón	239	1,201
Molina de Segura	4	24
Moratalla	8	24
Mula	31	127
Murcia	88	214
San Javier	811	3,695
La Manga del Mar Menor	749	3,523
within San Javier	62	172
San Pedro del Pinatar	104	317

You can see that the vast majority of apartments are available on the coast, with Cartagena and San Javier having the most (note that La Manga is split between these two government defined regions).

The casa rural market is very different (table below), showing that the inland region of the North West is most popular, with Moratalla way ahead and Caravaca de la Cruz following.

This split between rental types of apartments and casas rurales demonstrates the difference in the types of people likely to rent your property. Casas rurales will most likely attract Spanish nationals and other rural tourists, whereas apartments on the costas attract the more typical holidaymakers, looking for sun, sea and golf.

The vast majority of apartments are on the coast with Cartagena and San Javier having the most.

Number of Casas Rurales for Rent in Murcia (2006)

	Casas	Beds
TOTAL	448	2,913
Abanilla	6	32
Abarán	3	13
Águilas	2	16
Albudeite	0	0
Aledo	4	25
Alhama de Murcia	15	89
Archena	2	15
Blanca	19	107
Bullas	19	95
Calasparra	4	24

Casas rurales will most likely attract Spanish nationals and other rural tourists.

	Casas	Beds
Caravaca de la Cruz	71	525
Cartagena	6	37
Cehegín	25	145
Cieza	8	62
Fortuna	8	45
Fuente-Álamo	5	38
Jumilla	0	0
Lorca	18	117
Mazarrón	3	12
Molina de Segura	7	57
Moratalla	145	974
Mula	19	104
Murcia	7	53
Ojós	6	42
Pliego	3	14
Puerto Lumbreras	3	23
Ricote	7	62
San Javier	1	3
Torre Pacheco	4	24
Torres de Cotillas (Las)	1	6
Totana	13	72
Ulea	4	20
Villanueva del Río Segura	9	50
Yecla	1	12

RETIREMENT

After a life of working, what better way to enjoy your hard-earned rest than in a year-round, sunny, warm climate? There are health spas in places like Fortuna, Archena and the Mar Menor, providing specialised treatments plus many opportunities to partake in hobbies such as hiking, golf, painting, wildlife, sailing, fishing, history, watersports and more.

There are already many ex-pats here too so, even if your main reason for retiring in Murcia is the climate rather than the culture, a thriving social life is assured.

The retirement buyer has a wide range of choices; from houses and villas in the mini-villages (urbanisations) with all the leisure, health and retail amenities you need – to remote fincas where you can enjoy a slower pace of life in a traditional Spanish community.

Of course, if you're fit and able in retirement then a remote finca would be fine but if you're likely to need easy access to health centres or worry about security then a gated community or well equipped town would provide added peace of mind.

One final word of advice for homeowners thinking of selling up and relocating would be to see if you can rent your existing home out and remortgage that for a year or two while you give Spain a try. That way you will always have the option to return home later if you decide that Spain isn't for you after all.

Even if your main reason for retiring in Murcia is the climate rather than the culture, a thriving social life is assured.

Make Sure That Your Retirement in Spain is Financially Secure

If you chose to retire in Spain you are not alone. According to statistics from the UK's Department for Work and Pensions, Spain continues to be the most popular destination for British retirees who have chosen to live abroad. 74,000 people receive their British pension in Spain. 10 years ago the figure was only 26,700. Most people who make the move fully understand the attraction and very much enjoy their new life in Spain. Different people approach retirement with different emotions. Some don't look forward to it - worrying about having "nothing to do" with their time. Others eagerly anticipate having the free time to do whatever they please. They may have a list of pastimes they want to take up or lifetime ambitions they haven't had time to pursue yet.

I suspect that readers who retire in Spain fall in the latter category and embrace their retirement to the full! One downside of retirement though is the lack of a monthly salary. A pension is often not sufficient to maintain the lifestyle you are used to and you need to rely on your savings and investments. It is therefore essential for your long-term financial security to ensure that your money will last you for the rest of your life; keeping you at the level of comfort you are used to and with enough in the bank to cover unexpected expenses like medical bills and house repairs.

Statistically, people can expect to live 20 years in retirement; that's 20 years to enjoy your retirement dreams and life in Spain. Of course this is just an average; hopefully you'll have 30 or more years to enjoy. You'll have worked hard for your money and now is the time to start reaping the rewards - but you will need a careful plan to ensure you don't outlive your accumulated income.

There is nothing scarier than running out of money in your later years, especially if you are in a foreign country and don't have state welfare to fall back on. In any case, isn't it about time your money began working for you?

Choosing your retirement lifestyle

As a rule of thumb, those people wishing to continue living their pre-retirement lifestyle should expect their retirement expenses to be 80% of their current ones. This is because they have no costs associated with commuting to work, buying lunches every day and buying clothes for work etc. However, because you've moved to a new country your expenses will be different to those in the UK so you need to study the cost of living in Spain. In many ways life is cheaper in Spain, but if you take up new hobbies (for example golf or sailing) this can be expensive. You may also decide to travel more to see new countries, and simply going back and forth to the UK on regular visits to family and friends will add up, especially if you need to pay for hotels and car hire. It is also essential to ensure you have enough money set aside for emergencies.

Inflation

When I discuss financial planning with retirees they often state that they do not want to take any risk with their money. They reject many investments outright because their capital won't be protected. But I rarely hear anyone talk about the risks of inflation and yet this is one key risk retirees need to be aware of and plan to avoid.

Inflation should not be ignored. The fact is that when you leave your money in the bank (or a building society) it is not protected against inflation. This means that each year your money will be worth less and less. In other words, you can buy less with it next year than this year, even less the year after, even less the year after that etc etc.

Looking ahead 10 to 20 years, you will have lost a substantial portion of your money (it could be as much as 30-50%) in terms of how much it can buy you. Your deposit account will be earning interest, but much if not all of it will be wiped out by inflation, regardless of what your bank statement tells you. Leading economists in the UK argue that although the official rate of inflation has hit 3% in reality the real personal rate of inflation for the middle classes is 10%, and for pensioners it is 9%. It's similar in Spain – just look at how much things like petrol and health insurance have gone up. You would reject an investment where you'd lose 9%-10% each year, yet few people realise the dangers of leaving all their money on deposit.

I have met people who retired in the Costa del Sol 20 years ago, who thought they had plenty of money to live on for the rest of their life, and who today have run out of money to the point where they have had to sell their Spanish home and return to live with family in the UK. With appropriate planning you can prevent this happening to you.

Pensions

Depending on the type of pension you have and whether you have started drawing income from it, there may be ways to improve your pension fund and earn more from it. It's worth discussing your options with a financial adviser based in Spain, or one with thorough, up-to-date knowledge on Spanish regulations, who understands the law regarding pensions and how they are taxed in both the UK and Spain to see if more advantageous arrangements can be made.

Tax planning
If you want to protect your money you'll need to pay as little tax on it as possible. Please remember that in Spain you must declare and pay tax on your worldwide income and gains and you must declare bank interest earned in the Channel Islands and Isle of Man even if you are paying the withholding tax there. Failing to do so, for whatever reason, is a very risky strategy these days. It is more than likely that the Spanish authorities will find out about it at some point. However there are various ways you can structure your money to legitimately keep your tax obligations to the lowest possible. Tax rules and rates do change quite often and you need to keep on top of these to achieve the best possible tax advantages if you move Spain.

Estate planning
What will happen to your estate once you pass on? Will your beneficiaries be liable for inheritance tax in Spain and also possibly in the UK? Setting up an offshore trust would avoid this, as well as any problems with Spanish succession law. It would also speed up the probate process and ensure your money is distributed as per your instructions.

The majority of retirees want to feel that their money is secure and that they have enough income to live on comfortably. That is why the focus these days for those in retirement is wealth preservation and income provision.

Taking advice from an investments and tax expert is the first step towards this.

Bill Blevins
Managing Director of Blevins Franks, who offer financial advice for expats.
www.blevinsfranksinternational.com
UK: Jane Hayward ☎020 7015 2126 *jane.hayward@blevinsfranks.com*
Murcia: Neil Jenkins ☎965 705 502 *neil.jenkins@blevinsfranks.com*
www.blevinsfranks.com

RELOCATION

If you're moving to Murcia with your job then your target location may be limited to where your employer operates and how far your budget will stretch.

If you're just planning on moving to the region for a change of scenery and lifestyle then, within reason, anything goes. Although if you're likely to need a job pretty soon, it would make sense to learn Spanish first and ensure you're buying within an acceptable distance of a major employment hub such as a city, large town or resort.

Depending on whether you're single or moving with a family will also dictate your location choices. Good schools, security and a local social scene (especially for a trailing spouse) may be high on the agenda for a couple with children while proximity to nightlife, entertainment and good transport for work may be more important to a single buyer or young couple.

If you're likely to need a job pretty soon, it would make most sense to learn Spanish first and ensure you're buying within an acceptable distance of a major employment hub.

Expat Women
Helping Women Living Overseas

www.expatwomen.com is a free web site helping all expatriate women from all nationalities in any country in the world. You can share experiences and advice, find resources for living in a foreign country and get a monthly newsletter with success stories, mentor tips, reader experiences, book reviews and more.

stories - interviews - networking - support

Sign up FREE at...
www.expatwomen.com

Thinking of Moving Abroad?
Your Essential Considerations Covered

When you consider that the number of British retired persons living abroad now tops 1.3 million and that the rest of us Brits who are pre-retirees are spending tonnes of our money in well over forty countries in terms of buying property abroad, you can easily see that the lure of sunnier and more exotic climes affects a great many of us!

If you're thinking of moving abroad then you are certainly not alone – but there are certain essential considerations that you need to cover before you commit to relocation overseas. Additionally there are aspects of starting a new life abroad that you may not yet have thought about.

First things first, many people want to leave the UK behind simply because the climate can be so poor in Great Britain. That's as good a reason to leave as any especially if you have medical disorders exacerbated by the climate in the UK such as S.A.D or arthritis for example. But then you need to look carefully at the average climate month to month in your chosen overseas location of choice. Sure, Florida might look good right now – but it has hurricanes you know! Sure, Cyprus might be marketed as an island for all seasons but in January and February it rains more than it does in the UK and it gets very cold!

If you're moving abroad in retirement think about how far your pension income will stretch in your preferred overseas location – and find out whether your state entitlement will be frozen and your retirement income taxed – get forewarned about all of these facts.

If you're going to need to find a job overseas or you want to establish a business how likely is it that you will be successful in your endeavours?

Now think about the cost of living – yes, the UK is notoriously expensive for certain services and luxuries as well... so what about the nation you're moving to? How does the cost of living compare? Hopefully it's far less for day to day essentials but will you have to add on extra money for educating your children or taking out private healthcare?

Touching on both education and healthcare in the financial planning side of things is essential – but it's also wise to look a little more closely at available facilities and to determine whether these fall within your likely requirements and those of your family. If not, what are your alternatives? Will you have to move elsewhere or come back to the UK for medical attention? Will you have to privately educate your children back in the UK for example?

Other reasons that we Brits cite for leaving Blighty behind are lifestyle and the likes of rising crime statistics in the UK. Yes the British way of life can seem exhausting with the emphasis seemingly on living to work… so look abroad and find a place where the lifestyle more closely matches your own choices for the ways you live your life. With regards to crime – nowhere is crime free so be realistic, be safe and be fairly open minded!

When you move abroad you will have to adapt to a different culture and possibly a different language as well – if you have a strange penchant for xenophobia, chances are you'll find the move uncomfortable and strange and you'll never happily settle!

Take time out to rent a property abroad in your preferred country for at least a few months to ensure you really can adapt – do this even if you are the most open minded, tolerant and adaptable person. You never know whether the collective quirks of a given nationality will actually begin to rub you up the wrong way – and it's better to determine this before you've moved lock, stock and barrel really!

Also, know that if you're moving to a country where English is not widely spoken that you will really only get the most out of your relocation if you learn the mother tongue of your new neighbours and associates.

Something you will need to pay close attention to is the emotions you, your family and friends will go through regarding your move. You'll feel excitement and apprehension building up to the relocation and at some point in the first couple of years you'll feel an overwhelming senses of homesickness and regret mixed with highs and happiness. This process is normal and you'll get through it – but your family and friends may feel loss and regret when they see you leaving for your new life and you will have to work hard to keep links open and ties closely bound with regular visits 'back home' or with regular invites extended for your nearest and dearest to come and visit you.

Making new friends and enjoying new social experiences is one of the best aspects of moving abroad – so be prepared to embrace the experience with open arms. However, if you're shy and retiring you'll have to force yourself to get out and about otherwise how else will you discover all the interesting people out there?

Finally a word about real estate – property prices the world over have risen sharply in the past decade so look carefully at what your budget will enable you to buy. Think about the re-saleability of a property as well in case you ever want to move on or repatriate. Look at exchange rates, the buying process, cost of purchase and ownership of property and also the laws for foreign owners of property in your chosen nation. And then get a lawyer. Get your interests looked after and those of your successors because the rules of inheritance differ from nation to nation.

If you take time to review and think more deeply about these essential considerations with regards to your own personal situation then you will quickly find a way through the planning and preparing and you'll be well on your way to starting a new life abroad from a position of far deeper understanding of everything involved in the entire relocation process.

Rhiannon Williamson
www.shelteroffshore.com

Home Comforts

For those of you for whom learning a new language is daunting and you are really looking at Murcia's sunshine as its principal benefit, there are plenty of opportunites.

From the coastal new-build housing estates and Campos de Golf, to the villages that have a high ex-pat population, home comforts can be found aplenty.

Within the newly-built housing estates you can find a range of properties from one bedroom apartments through to 4 bedroom detached houses, with as many bathrooms and a swimming pool too! Almost all of the new housing estates built for non-Spaniards have an en-suite golf course. In addition most estates have shops catering for all the expat needs, including expat staff and goods you'll only be able to get back home.

You'll also find bars and restaurants selling British or Irish beer by the pint, pie and chips, fry ups and other such British gourmet fare!

There are plenty of social clubs in Murcia, set up by and catering for Brits – from bridge to badminton; cricket to crochet!

Areas with large expat communities are indicated in the location guide.

Areas with large expat communities are indicated in the location guide. Whether you choose to buy here or avoid expat areas altogether is a personal choice.

HOLIDAY/SECOND HOME

Depending upon your holiday tastes – Murcia has it all. From city breaks to complete isolation – traditional Spanish culture to a (somewhat sunnier) home away from home.

If the holiday home is for you then there's no right answer here but obviously you'll want to choose a location that you're not going to be tired of returning to year after year.

If you're looking for a property that you will only sporadically occupy then it's a good idea to buy somewhere with high regular occupancy. This will ensure people are around to watch over your home, and minimise your fear of bandits, raiding and looting (a real concern in more remote rural areas).

Also, many people think they'll buy a holiday home and cover the mortgage payments by renting out to friends and family. If this is the case then be prepared to sacrifice some of your tastes to ensure people will want to stay there. You *might* love the idea of living in a cave 20km away from the nearest civilisation for a week but most other holidayers might prefer something a bit more orthodox – such as a place by the sea with a pool.

Also bear in mind that if you are going to rent out your home to other people they're likely to want it during the peak season, which may mean you'll only get your chance when it's raining, and everything's closed.

> *Bear in mind that if you are going to rent out your home to other people they're likely to want it during the peak season, which may mean you'll only get your chance when everything's closed.*

Location, location, location but not without Preparation, preparation, preparation...

Yes, the location, location, location theory has been well documented and is of course a very important part of the moving process. But, even more important, when leaving your home country for a move abroad you cannot afford to overlook preparation and planning of your proposed move.

If you haven't done your homework before selling up lock stock and barrel you will be in for a rough ride; only the toughest survive and the strain it can put on a relationships is tough, even harder if you have a family in tow.

For those who read this that are thinking of moving to Spain, I would like to give you a few practical tips to help you succeed – especially when it comes to preparation.

- Give yourself as much time as practically possible before your planned move.
- Read books about moving to Spain and investigate on the internet.
- Outline all your reasons for moving to Spain, write them down and then try to find out where abouts in Spain fits all your needs and desires.
- Try and narrow down 3 or 4 areas that tick the YES box for most of your requirements.
- If you can, and this might be difficult and expensive if you have a family, take a trip of about a week or so to discover if your choices come up to scratch in reality. Go out of the holiday season (Oct/Nov).
- If you are going to be buying property, make sure you do your sums correctly and get professional, independent, financial advice.
- Think about how you are going to support yourself, financially.
- Take Spanish language lessons.
- Before you rush into buying you might want to think about renting for a while.

These are just a number of things you can do to help avoid the pitfalls, insecurity and language barriers when moving to Spain. It is possible to come up against some real trouble with bureaucracy, ignorance and conflicting information as well as lack of knowledge on specific matters, within some local authorities and government departments when moving to Spain.

With all of that said once you come to terms with how things work in Spain, learn not to expect things to happen as you are used to and join in the relaxed mañana way of life I do not think you will regret it! The quality of life that you can have in Spain for you and your family can be truly fantastic.

As for the Preparation, well, I know from experience no matter how much and how well you prepare there is always going to be something happen that you just cannot predict but the more time you put into the preparation of moving to Spain, the easier your life will become when integrating into the Spanish culture and way of life.

Paul Shoulders
www.spanish-sol-utions.com

What Should You Buy?

RENOVATION

If you want to make a quick return on your investment then adding value to a property by renovating it can be a good way to go. Renovated townhouses in popular locations with a traditional old-town, such as Moratalla for instance, will achieve almost double the asking price of their slightly run-down neighbours.

The most important thing to do before buying a property to renovate is to check permissions with an architect and the townhall.

If you're buying a Finca with loads of land and have a plan to build your dream villa on it make sure this will be allowed first. Otherwise you'll have lots of land and end up living in a caravan!

Renovated townhouses in popular locations with a traditional old-town will achieve almost double the asking price of their slightly run-down neighbours.

SELF-BUILD

There are opportunities to purchase land and build your own ideal home. Land prices are increasing and availability is reducing, however this is still an option for some people. Take great care and get excellent legal advice before embarking upon this route as planning permissions vary throughout the region.

with new developments springing up all the time, older properties have to compete with shiny new ones and as a result are likely to achieve a lower sales price.

NEW-BUILD AND OFF-PLAN

There are plenty of new builds becoming available, either off-plan or to be bought before they've been lived in (ie buy from an investor). The benefits include having some say in the interior finish (tiles, bathroom suite etc.) and owning a brand new house. The cons include the potentially ever-moving goal posts for completion and the worry about possible price decreases during the waiting time.

However, many savvy investors have successfully "flipped" a new build purchase, selling before occupation at good profit. This is a risky strategy and not for the feint hearted.

All along the golf valley (C3319 motorway) and around Alhama de Murcia there are plenty of new urbanisations with off-plan properties.

RESALE (SECOND HAND)

If buying second hand on a resort or urbanisation you will be able to get a good idea of the popularity of the location and the quality of amenities and maintenance – which is something you don't get if buying new-build and off-plan.

However, with new developments springing up all the time, older properties have to compete with shiny new ones and as a result are likely to achieve a lower sales price.

This is good news for the buyer as you won't be paying the "new house" premium that the previous buyer did and so are less likely to lose money in the future.

Other types of resale property can include fincas, villas, townhouses and city apartments, which are in generally good condition. My advice is to shop around and aim to pay less; plenty of new properties mean it's a buyer's market so don't be afraid to put in a cheeky offer!

OFF-PLAN VERSUS SECOND HAND

How do you decide whether to buy off-plan or second hand? You've probably heard of people who've made a small fortune by buying off-plan and they never even moved in! Well it really depends upon your level of risk aversion and your plans. Below are some of the pros and cons of each; it's up to you to decide which strategy will be best for you and your circumstances.

Advantages of Off-Plan

Investment – By purchasing very early in the construction phase (or even before construction has begun) you can make a good investment. Initially the prices are set below market value to attract investors, which helps the developer finance the construction, so you might be able to resell the property at a profit before completion.

Initially prices are set below market value to attract investors.

Selection - By purchasing at an early stage it is possible to choose the best properties i.e. with the best views, penthouse, corner etc.

Guarantee - New buildings include a 10-year guarantee for main failures in the structure, roof, etc.

First Owner - You are the first to occupy the property and can therefore personalise it as you wish. You don't have to pay to change things the previous owner has installed and you shouldn't have any nasty surprises.

Availability - There is a wide choice on offer with many off-plan properties available in Murcia at many of the new developments.

Price - The prices for new developments are set by professional developers who have a much greater knowledge of the market value (compared to private sellers) and you will therefore not find major variations in prices for off-plan properties of the same standard. The difference in price is reflected by other factors such as the standard/quality of the development, the location, views, etc.

The lowest priced off-plans available at the time of writing are for around €100,000, for apartments on Santa Ana (Jumilla) and La Tercia (in the Golf Valley). The highest prices are €600,000+ at Condado de Alhama and €500,000 at Hacienda del Álamo.

The lowest priced off-plans available at the time of writing are around €100,000 for apartments on Santa Ana (Jumilla) and La Tercia (in the Golf Valley).

Disadvantages of Off-Plan

Viewing - When you buy off-plan you will not be able to see the finished product (the property) until the completion of the construction.

Waiting Time - To be able to get a good and cheap property under construction you will have to buy early which, of course, means that you will have to wait a long time before your property is finished. This could be anything from 6 months to 6 years!

Changes - The area around the development can change. Although you inspect the plot where your property is going to be built you don't know how the area is going to develop during and after the construction. Your lawyer should look at the local town plan for the area, although new building licenses can still be given after you decide to purchase.

Late Purchaser - If you buy a property under construction in the final phase then the investment value will be significantly lower than an early purchase and the best properties will have been sold.

Delays – Probably the biggest concern. A high percentage of all new constructions in Spain are delayed either because of bad planning or because of some problems with getting the final licenses. The best way to make sure this doesn't happen is to buy from respected developers and to make sure there is a penalty in the contract in case of delays.

The popular press enjoy a good horror story when it comes to delays of new builds. Whilst there are often cases when a development is behind schedule, a well-written contract should keep you safe. Always ensure you have a bank guarantee and penalty clauses.

Bankruptcy – By using a good, impartial lawyer you should be able to protect yourself from this eventuality, however, this is often a concern for buyers. Make sure that a bank guarantee and insurance are in place. Also ensure that all the rest of the papers are in order such as building licenses etc. as these are the most frequent reasons why a construction is not completed.

Not What You Expected – the build quality isn't what you expected, or the finish isn't up to your standards. Make sure you do a full quality assurance checklist before making your final payment.

Advantages of Second Hand

Less Waiting - When you buy a second hand property the waiting time to complete the purchase is much less than when buying a property under construction. If the seller agrees it is possible to complete the purchase at the notary as soon as the buyer has the money ready and his lawyer has gone through all the paperwork.

Negotiable Prices - Although the investment value on average is lower compared to buying off-plan at an early stage it is still possible to find a good buy and it is almost always possible to negotiate the price.

Viewing - It is possible to visit the actual property (and more than once if necesarry) to make sure that it is the right property and to go through and inspect all the nooks and crannies.

It is almost always possible to negotiate the price of second hand property.

Availability - The availability of second hand properties is more varied than off-plan developments. You can find everything from old properties (fincas, apartments, townhouses etc.) that need complete renovation, to furnished and ready to move into properties. Furthermore there are many areas (i.e. the city centre, the country etc.) where the only option is a second hand property as it is very difficult or impossible to find new developments because of lack of space or new building restrictions.

Disadvantages of Second Hand

Finding the Right Property - As every second hand property is different it normally takes a long time and many visits to different properties to find the right one for you.

No Guarantee - There are no guarantees on second hand properties. If there is any damage to the property after you have bought it you will be responsinble for fixing it.

Agent Fees - Second hand properties are normally sold through estate agents. Although many agents provide a very good service their involvement will increase the price of the property; the commission of the agent is normally put on top of the price the seller wants.

Price - The prices on second hand properties are set directly by the private seller and there is a great variation in price from property to property within the same area.

If there is any damage to a second hand property after you have bought it you will be responsinble for fixing it.

Where Should You Buy?

CITY

The majority of people living in Murcian cities and more modern towns live in apartments. This seems to be an aspirational lifestyle choice though many people also aspire to owning a weekend hideaway in the countryside or near the sea!

Choose your district with extreme care however. Spending some time in the locality to get to know it well will pay off in the long run and will also help you avoid making expensive mistakes. I highly recommend renting in the area you're thinking of buying in first.

Living in the city in summer can be noisy – so if you're considering a city home then be prepared to sleep with earplugs! Youngsters on mopeds, with helmets on elbows, and the late night revelrie that accompanies most Spanish cities can be exhausting for some. Of course others may wish to join in!

Choose your district with extreme care. Spending some time in the area will pay off in the long run and will also help you avoid making expensive mistakes.

Ideal for...

- People moving to Murcia, who still need to work for a living and need regular access to the conveniences of modern city living.

- Investors looking for long-term rental income – possibly from the local Spanish market.

- Developers/Investors who want to charge a premium for selling properties to the aspirational city-living market.

Pros...

- ✓ Good long-term rental market – in the right places.
- ✓ Convenient range of shops, services and transport links.
- ✓ Easy connection to services such as water, electricity, telephone and internet.

Cons...

- ✗ Higher noise, congestion and pollution.
- ✗ Expect to get less actual property for your money.
- ✗ High crime in some areas compared to rural locations.
- ✗ Traffic and parking at the wrong times can be a nightmare.
- ✗ You're really limited in your choice to either Murcia or Cartagena (though Lorca and Águilas are growing).

If you want city properties in Murcia then you are really limited to either Murcia or Cartagena.

TOWN

There are parts of Murcia that have yet to be inundated with expats and these are the places where you will need to speak Spanish; your neighbours will be Spanish, the shops will be owned and run by Spanish people and most of your friends will only speak Spanish.

Whether you choose to buy in a functional town with a good local property market or whether your goal is to buy a beautiful renovation project in one of Murcia's many pretty, traditional winding towns there is plenty to choose from.

By selecting this option you will not only benefit from the wonderful climate of Murcia but also from the rich and fantastic culture. If you're buying to live in Murcia and looking for a real change and challenge then this is the way to go.

You must be prepared to work hard at integrating into your new community though and learning Spanish should be your priority.

Of course some towns and villages have a high population of expats so you can still get a taste of real Spain but with the benefits of other like-languaged people nearby. Use the location-o-meter in the location section to help you find them.

Some towns and villages have a high population of expats so you can still get a taste of real Spain but with the benefits of other like-languaged people nearby.

Ideal for...
- Functional towns make ideal bases for people who want the benefits of good local facilities but with the countryside on their doorstep.
- People who are moving abroad for the first time and want to ease themselves into real Spain.

Pros...
✓ Convenient range of shops, services and (in some cases) transport links.

✓ Easy connection to services such as water, electricity, telephone and internet.

✓ Beautiful countryside on your doorstep.

✓ Lower prices than in cities and on resorts.

Cons...
✗ If you don't speak Spanish you could be in for a shock in many towns!

✗ Long-term rental market will be slower in all but the most popular working towns.

✗ Holiday rental market – especially inland - may not be as consistent as resorts near the coast.

If you don't speak Spanish you could be in for a shock.

COUNTRYSIDE

Renovations, fincas, village and townhouses can all be found in the campo here. In fact it's possible to find properties that are upto 20km away from the nearest civilisation. Often they will be up country tracks, with subsequent challenges in reaching them!

Living remotely brings its own benefits and challenges. You can get fantastic views and peace but the drawbacks include fixing punctures on your car and the lack of some services like water, electricity and drainage, which you will have to make arrangements for yourself.

In Murcia you may well find that you need to take special care that these properties are not in protected areas or within national parks. The best way to discover this is by asking an independent architect.

There are also properties within just a few kilmoteres of charming villages where you get the best of all worlds; peace and quite but with easy access to services and the village lifestyle.

Many Murcian villages have traditional single story houses, most of which were built about 100 years ago, with a central reception area and doors leading off to bedrooms, living rooms and a kitchen. They are usually dimly lit, with small windows and thick walls for warmth in winter and coolness in summer.

Many Murcian villages have traditional single story houses with a central reception area and doors leading off to bedrooms, living rooms and a kitchen.

Ideal for...

- People looking for a more peaceful, but infinitley more challenging, way of life in real Spain.

- Retirees who want their own private slice of paradise in a warm climate with beautiful views.

Pros...

✓ Wonderful scenery and beautiful nature all around.

✓ Lots of house/land for your money.

✓ Peace and quiet.

Cons...

✗ Planning/Building permission may be impossible in some areas – don't ever trust the estate agent on what can and can't be done - always check for yourself.

✗ That wonderful view could be ruined if a new golf resort or housing estate gets the go-ahead in the future.

✗ Peace and tranquillity could be lost if a new road or airport is built nearby.

✗ Simple things like water, electricity, telephone and drainage are often not simple at all out in the campo.

✗ Access to some remote property is pretty poor – expect punctures, buckled wheels, wonky exhausts and, in particularly rainy periods, no car access at all.

Countryside properties are ideal for people looking for a more peaceful – yet challenging – way of life in real Spain.

COAST/BEACH RESORT

For those who crave daily access to their own stretch of beach there are some fantastic beachside towns with an authentic Spanish feel such as Águilas. There are also a small number of existing houses near the protected coastlines where newbuilds are prohibited.

Other than these areas your options are going to be limited to apartments in the highrises on the La Manga stip, urbanizations along the Costa Cálida and resorts a little way inland.

Murcia has hopefully learned from the mistakes of other over-developed parts of Spain and has introduced building restrictions which should help safeguard most of the coastline here from turning into a high-rise hell.

Murcia has introduced building restrictions which should help prevent the coastline here from turning into a high-rise hell.

Ideal for...

- Holiday rental – with good, almost yearlong prospects.

- Investors – coastal property will always be popular and in the more protected areas where newbuilds are prohibited properties can attract a premium.

- Retirees – if sunbathing, coastal walks and the sea inspire you then the coast will be your ideal retirement spot.

- Relocaters – if you want to find work in tourism, bars and entertainment then this is as good a coast as any.

Pros...
- ✓ Long rental periods – ideal for holiday investment.
- ✓ Plenty of leisure and dining facilities on the coast to cater for tourists.
- ✓ Good job market for people happy to work in hotels, bars and restaurants etc
- ✓ The beach is one of the best places to enjoy all that Murcian sun.

Cons...
- ✗ It can get very busy and the character, and population, of some towns changes beyond all recognition in peak season.
- ✗ You'll get much less property/land for your money than further in land.
- ✗ Parking and congestion can be a nightmare in peak season.

The character and population of some coastal towns can change beyond all recognition in peak season.

URBANIZATION/GOLF RESORT

Most of the areas in Murcia have existing housing developments – usually built for the foreign investment market. Some are very well established and popular such as La Manga Club, which was one of the original urbanisations.

The more mature urbanisations usually have their infrastructure in place with well-developed amenities, completed road systems, lush, green golf courses and the cranes and heavy machinery removed. However, this isn't always the case. In addition existing urbanisations are expanding and building work has begun again, if it ever stopped, on some of the most popular ones.

It's also possible that the older estates will be starting to look a little shabby round the edges.

For new developments in the location section, where known I've included the name of the developer and a website address or telephone number. However, for purchases you will probably need to go through one of their agents. Most developers have a number of agents and you'll find a full list of agents in the resources section.

The proliferation of new builds, especially around the city of Murcia, in the Campo de Cartagena (The Golf Valley) and some of the larger cities (Lorca for example) means there are many opportunities for an off plan purchase or a new build. There are also many resales on these developments of properties that have not even been lived in.

There is a tendency to turn the larger developments into mini towns, including everything from schools, universities, and hospitals to hotels, restaurants, commercial areas and sporting complexes.

There is a tendency to turn the larger developments into mini towns, including everything from schools, universities, hospitals, hotels, restaurants, commercial areas and sporting complexes (not just the golf) and private security firms. Of course, most self-respecting new urbanisations have an 18-hole golf course, designed by a famous golfer (or footballer!)

Many of the new developments are being actively marketed to the Spanish population and some boast excellent take up from this home sector. One of the major benefits of Spanish purchasers is the potential for year round occupancy, avoiding the ghost town issues that plague some of the popular expat developments.

Water scarcity is still a major hurdle in the region however, which brings much criticism for the many water-thirsty golf resorts springing up. The more conscientious (and PR minded) developers are including their own desalination plants and other elaborate water management systems to overcome this.

New laws in the Murcia region insist that 100% of the infrastructure (roads, services etc.) is in place before building licenses are granted. This should help you avoid the problem of buying an off-plan house only to find it remains marooned in a wasteland with electricity 2km away for many years to come!

New laws in the Murcia region insist that 100% of the infrastructure is in place before building licenses are granted.

Ideal for...
- Holiday rental - thanks to almost year-round golf!
- Investors - golf and sunshine is popular!
- Retirees - if golf is your thing and you want to be near other expats.

Pros...
✓ Long rental periods - ideal for holiday investment.
✓ Plenty of leissure and dining facilities being built on most urbanisations.

Buying Property in Murcia

- ✓ Many of the new urbanisations will include their own health facilites and schools.
- ✓ Good job market in bars, restaurants and leisure facilities etc.

Cons...

- ✗ As so many properties are packed into these urbanisations there will be a lot of competition for renters.
- ✗ You'll get much less property/land for your money.
- ✗ You need to rely on others to keep your investment safe and secure.

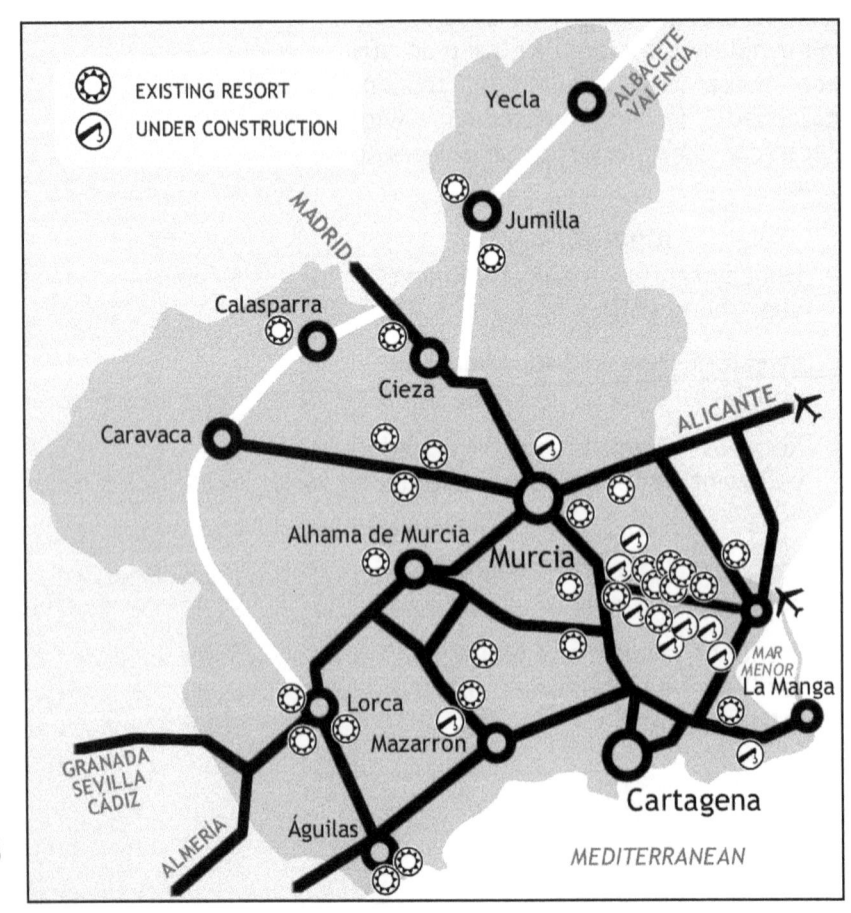

Buying Process

BUYING IN MURCIA - AT-A-GLANCE

The following flowcharts give you an overview of the complete buying process from start to finish and can be used as your at-a-glance progress checklist and sanity checker.

- Step 1: At Home – Planning and Research
- Step 2: In Murcia – Research Trip (1 week)
- Step 3: At Home – Organise Inspection Trip
- Step 4: In Murcia – Inspection Trip (2 weeks)
- Step 5: At Home – Get The Money
- Step 6: In Murcia – Finalise Purchase

Buying Property in Murcia

Step 1: At Home – Planning and Research

Decide Why You're Buying
- ☐ Investment
- ☐ Rental
- ☐ Holidays
- ☐ For Family
- ☐ To Live

↓

Determine Budget
- ☐ Mortgage/remortgage
- ☐ Staged financing
- ☐ Credit Cards
- ☐ Sell something/cash in stocks or options
- ☐ Get Financial Advice

↓

Do Research
- ☐ Read – this guidebook
- ☐ Internet – resources at end – look up estate agents, abogados, gestors, architects etc
- ☐ Decide which towns to shortlist. Use section 1 of this guidebook
- ☐ Recommendations – from friends, bulletin boards, magazines

↓

Make Criteria
Where? ☐town ☐village ☐seaside ☐mountains ☐countryside ☐urbanisation
Transport? ☐driving ☐trains ☐airports ☐motorways
Amenities? ☐hospitals ☐schools ☐colleges ☐nightlife ☐restaurants & bars
Type? ☐restoration ☐new build ☐off plan ☐pre-owned

↓

Make Specification
Size? ☐bedrooms ☐bathrooms ☐garage
Outdoor space? ☐garden ☐patio ☐pool ☐trees

↓

Arrange Research Trip
- ☐ Flights
- ☐ Accommodation
- ☐ Travel
- ☐ Meetings – Agent, Abogado, Gestor, Architect etc.

Visit Short-listed Town/Area
- ☐ Check amenities
- ☐ Visit Estate Agents
- ☐ Visit Developers / Collect details of properties
- ☐ Meet up with private vendors
  (people selling their own properties or Corredor)
- ☐ Meet Abogados, Gestors & Architects

repeat as necessary

Step 2: In Murcia - Research Trip

Check In Point
Is this still what you want to do?
Is this still the right area?
Are your criteria correct?
Is your specification reasonable?
Is your budget adequate?

Money
- ☐ Ensure money is available & accessible (approx 15% of your budget)
- ☐ Select bank and make appointment to open account (need passport)

Arrange Inspection Trip
- ☐ Flights
- ☐ Accommodation - hotel / B&B / Casa Rural
- ☐ Travel
- ☐ Meetings - Estate Agents / Vendors / Developers - send or tell them your criteria and ensure they have properties to match!
- ☐ Meetings - Abogados / Architects
- ☐ Meeting - Gestor to get an NIE
  (need passport & 2 photos)

Step 3: At Home - Organise Inspection Trip

Buying Property in Murcia

Step 4: In Murcia – Inspection Trip

Accompanied Viewings
- ☐ Be clear on criteria
- ☐ Be flexible
- ☐ Take camera and video camera – take lots of photos and video footage to help decide later
- ☐ Take GPS coordinates – especially for rural properties
- ☐ Make notes

Make Short List
- ☐ Go to bar and compare each property against original criteria
- ☐ Deselect any obvious properties
- ☐ Have a big drink!
- ☐ Revisit properties alone – use the GPS coordinates!
- ☐ Meet with neighbours
- ☐ Check out local amenities
- ☐ Discuss with Abogado – is the paperwork correct, are they able to sell it, is it what & where you thought it was, does the nota simple look right?
- ☐ Discuss with Architect – can you do renovations, building works, is it architecturally sound, what are the likely costs involved?

Check In Point
Is this still what you want to do?
Is this still the right area?
Are your criteria correct?
Is your specification reasonable?
Is your budget adequate?

Choose Property
- ☐ Make offer
- ☐ Sign contract
- ☐ Give deposit – usually 10%
- ☐ Set up bank account – Gestor can help
- ☐ Set up Post Office box for correspondence
- ☐ Organise NIE – Gestor can do this
- ☐ Select Abogado – choose an English-speaking solicitor and instruct them
- ☐ Have a bigger drink – you've just bought a property!

Get Money
- ☐ Make arrangements to acquire the necessary money
- ☐ Transfer money to bank account in Spain

Wait
- ☐ Abogado will tell you when paperwork is ready

Arrange Buying Trip
- ☐ Flights
- ☐ Accommodation - hotel / B&B / Casa Rural
- ☐ Travel

Completion
- ☐ Visit Abogado agent who will tell you plans
- ☐ Go to bank and order money - probably cheque and cash
- ☐ Go to bank and withdraw cash and get cheque
- ☐ Notario appointment (usually arranged by Abogado)
- ☐ Read through all documents in presence of Notario & sellers
- ☐ Hand over cheque
- ☐ Notario turns away - hand over cash portion
- ☐ Sign LOTS of documents
- ☐ Receive keys - congratulations, you've finalised your property purchase

Receive Deeds (Escritura)
- ☐ 6-12 months after purchase

Step 5: At Home - Get Money

Step 6: In Murcia - Finalise Purchase

Who Does What?

DEVELOPER

As with property developers in the UK, property developers in Spain are on to a good thing. The first Hummer 4x4 I saw in Murcia was driven by a property developer, need I say more?

Even if you are buying on a large development you are very unlikely to deal direct with the developer as they will invariably employ the services of (often several competing) local selling agents. Their main job is to acquire land, get plans drawn up, build and then get their properties sold.

VENDOR

While many private vendors will also use an estate agent many will still be open to selling direct. If, and only if, you have a really good command of the Spanish language and have spent years in Spain, should you consider going 'off piste' and buying privately. However, never, ever shake hands, pay anything or commit to anything before you have engaged the services of a local solicitor. The vendor will treat this with a great deal of suspicion since "that's not how they would do it" and "they aren't necessary and are a waste of money and time." You need to play dumb and just say you need them to translate the paperwork for you and to understand the process. Usually the vendor will already be well-known to your future neighbours and probably related to them so it pays to be nice.

Never, ever shake hands, pay anything or commit to anything before you have engaged the services of a local solicitor.

ESTATE/SELLING AGENT

Estate agents in Murcia are little different from those elsewhere – that means, as a rule, they're not to be given your trust until they've earned it!

While this sounds unfair you have to remember that their goal is to sell the property they are representing and, as such, it's in their and their client's interests for them to accentuate the positives and, where possible, distract your attention away from the negatives.

Of course there are always exceptions and I know and have dealt with some fantastic, ethical and professional agents. However, I've also dealt with far too many who were "a bit dodgy" to say the least!

Estate agents take an even greater cut of the sale in Spain so will often pursue a sales lead with rabid persistence. Therefore many local estate agents perceive foreign buyers as having more money than sense.

As I said, there *are* good estate agents who are will look after your interests as well as their own, just not too many of them! Make sure you check out the history of an estate agent. Visit their offices, meet the staff and most importantly ask for references.

As well as an area-by-area listing of agents in the Resources section of this book you can look on the internet and in the local expat press for their adverts and local papers such as La Verdad for buying in the cities.

The local Spanish press has run some amusing articles on how some of the estate agents operating in the region can totally misrepresent what's being sold, and put on a price tag that no local Spaniard in their right mind would consider.

DreamSpain

Visit our website to find your dream home on all the major developments in Murcia or call for a friendly and professional english speaking service.

UK 0845 86 200 50
Spain 0034 626 544 987
www.dreamspain.net

Your Spanish Property Agent

Your Spanish property agent should have a positive impact on your experience of buying property in Spain. But as a buyer there are a few steps you should take to make sure you get the very best out of your agent.

The first step is to find an agent you can trust. Not a sales representative driven by targets but a dedicated property agent who has extensive experience of the area and properties. Recommendation is key but, failing that, search for a specialist in your chosen region then ask to talk to previous clients. Make sure you speak to the actual agent that is going to show you property so they can start to assess your needs. The relationship with your agent normally has two phases, pre and post sale. Unfortunately some agents try to charge for the latter stage, but stick to your guns and find an agent that recognises both are an essential part of their role.

With this aspect safely secured, you have to do something which many people find understandably uncomfortable – be completely open with your agent. Most of us have a natural and very sensible cynicism towards anyone trying to sell us anything – but if you've chosen your agent well you should be able to show them the inner workings of your mind and give them a good indication of the size of your pocket without fear.

An agent should not be selling to you but helping you, sharing with you the nuggets of their experience and the benefit of their local contacts and network.

Debate with your agent exactly why you want to buy a property in Spain. If it's primarily for investment, but you also hope it will improve your golf handicap then say so. Or if you really want a holiday home but also see it as a nest egg for your grandchildren then don't hold back. Why you are buying the property and how you are intending to use it can shape the advice they give you. Indeed if you are not clear on the type of property you want then one of the best approaches is to talk purely about how you will use it. Will you be inviting family to join you? Is it somewhere for summer or winter holidays or do you intend to use it to generate extra income?

Budget also needs to be discussed. There is little point turning your budget into a quiz show where your agent has to guess what you can afford. You will only end up seeing properties either physically or financially unsuitable and wasting your own precious viewing time.

Be realistic, set yourself a limit and ask your agent not to show you property above that limit – you do not want to buy a dream property only for it to turn into a financial nightmare. Talk openly about how you will raise your finance. Usually agents will have contacts with local banks that can offer competitive loans. This could all take place before you leave your home country, however, you may feel better in face to face discussion – often over a good cup of Spanish coffee.

When you begin your viewing visit your agent will probably have two lists of properties. Those you have picked and another list they jotted down from listening to you. View properties from both lists and work together to narrow the choice down. As you start to view property you'll build up 'must have' and 'don't want' criteria. If you are not interested in a property, say so! No one will be offended, you can move quickly to the next property and your agent can probably add or discount a few others from the list based on your comments.

When you decide on a specific property ask your agent if there is any room for negotiation. On resale properties they should already have a good idea if the owner will accept offers, but on new build properties the price is usually non-negotiable. Ask if they are able to negotiate a little on payment terms or offer you a financial incentive themselves – it all helps.

Always engage a solicitor. Your agents can normally recommend one but do check the solicitor is independent from your builder. If your circumstances ever change, proper independent legal advice is invaluable.

Once you've secured your property you may now be looking at an agent relationship, which could stretch over several years. Specify now how this relationship should develop and how much or little contact you would like. Remember, your agent is there for you, and working together is the key to a smooth property purchase.

Martine Cherry
www.dreamspain.net

CORREDOR

A corredor is usually a private individual working in the role as an estate agent and will be taking a similar cut to estate agents. They are often gregarious characters, who can usually be contacted via the main bar in the town. There is almost always a family connection with any property they sell. As with estate agents their first priority is to sell the property so do your own checks and harbour a healthy cynicism for anything they tell you.

ABOGADO

These are Spanish solicitors and in the city of Murcia it's usually possible to find one who speaks English. By comparison to UK solicitors you'll be pleasantly surprised by the reasonableness of their fees. They never usually expect cash up front and will bill when the work is complete.

However, their knowledge of the law may only extend to the rules in their part of the region and there is huge variation in regional government in Murcia. So, while you can't expect your solicitor to immediately understand all of the peculiarities of an area you should expect them to go away and find out!

Solicitors' fees in Spain are surprisingly reasonable by UK standards.

GESTOR

A Gestor is essentially a "gofer" – a licensed runner, who knows all the ins and outs of the paperwork and your local town hall. They can jump to the front of queues in Ayuntamientos, while lesser mortals wait for hours. They are invaluable for saving you time, stress and hassle dealing with lots of paperwork and not just purchasing the property.

NOTARIO

A notario is mandatory in Spain and must be used when buying a property. They are equivalent to a local UK magistrate and their main role in life is to stamp bits of paperwork to ensure the sale of the property can be completed.

Gestors can jump to the front of queues in Ayuntamientos while the rest of us have to wait for hours.

La táctica del palo y la zanahoria - The stick and the carrot - Spanish property

A few years ago, unwittingly trapped in a Spanish timeshare presentation I witnessed the sales director showing us his carrot - a week on a fancy cruise ship for those that bought a life subscription to a week's hotel accommodation. At the time I couldn't believe how people were agreeing to part with thousands of pounds in the space of minutes to ensure they got their free one-off cruise. I had clearly seen the strength of the carrot. For those who wavered the stick then appeared - not only would they lose the carrot (cruise) but the timeshare price was unrepeatable - they were going to miss the offer of a lifetime - for them it was now or never!

Times have moved on since then and people are buying whole properties in Spain rather than just a week of the year. However both the carrot and stick are still here with us and I'm surprised how often they are unfortunately still used.

The biggest carrot dangled to prospective buyers right now is the free or cheap inspection trip. These trips were once nothing more than three days of intense sales tactics until the buyer caved in and put down a deposit but this has improved and clients are handled with softer gloves. Although it is worth bearing in mind that these pre-paid trips put pressure on companies to get a higher closure rate which in turn leads to increased pressure on you to buy.

A wiser move is to book an inspection trip where money is returned if and after you have bought - no financial risk equals less reason to exert even the most subtle pressure on you and you are more likely to be shown properties which suit your requirements rather than the sales target.

The stick still appears when doubt strikes, usually in the shape of 'the last property available', or other 'eager' buyers. Often only a couple of hours are allowed to hold a property and pay a deposit.

Now properties in Murcia and the Costa Cálida have been selling quickly in recent years, so there are cases when this is a valid warning if you are looking for something specific. However, usually you should be able to make a commitment free reservation to give yourself time to think before you part with any money or put your name to the contract. Which raises another good point – you must have your solicitor check any contract before you sign your name on the dotted line. You are making a big financial commitment so don't be afraid to say "¡Para el carro!" which equates to "hold your horses" and take some time to think through your decision, get the details checked and steer clear of companies using emotional enticement or duress.

Martine Cherry
www.dreamspain.net

Essentials

NIE

Número de Identificación de Estranjero – this document is for resident and non-resident foreigners, acting as a social security number. You will need this to open a bank account and for other major purchases.

BANK ACCOUNT

A bank account in Spain is required for legal reasons and to access the large quantities of cash you will need to complete the transaction. It is very easy to do – select your bank, take your passports and NIEs and some Euros and it will be completed within minutes. Your bank cards and cheque book turn up some weeks later to your PO box (see below).

Charges in Spanish banks can be exorbitant and they are wide ranging. In Murcia, the Caja Rural is a popular choice for Brits, as their charges are incredibly low for transfers, and in some of the larger branches they have English-speaking staff.

MONEY

You will need banker's drafts and wads of cash for most transactions during the buying process and cash machines in Spain frequently charge you even more than they do in the UK if you withdraw your cash from a competitor's bank.

You will need a NIE to open a bank account and for other major purchases.

ESCRITURA

These are the equivalent to the deeds to your property. It's a set of original documents, which are signed and sealed by notaries, ayuntamiento and in some cases the seller and buyer. Usually you'll receive this document a few months after completion, after it has done the rounds at the ayuntamiento!

You should treat your Escritura carefully, keep it in a safe place – in the bank for example.

Look after your Escritura and put it in a safe place.

NOTA SIMPLE

This is closer to the equivalent of the land registry document in the UK and is usually available for download by your abogado from the central Spanish registry via the internet.

It's always good to have a few copies of this after you've bought as you can use it to demonstrate your ownership of the property, for getting padrón (your electoral role), or buying a car.

Nota Simples are easy to make photocopies of and are accepted as proof of ownership by most organisations.

Photocopies of Nota Simples are accepted as proof of ownership in most places.

LAND REGISTRY

There are two property registries – *Catastro* (land registry) and *Registro de la Propriedad* (property registry).

If you are buying a property with a plot (as opposed to an urbanisation) then your property will most likely be registered with both bodies.

Confirm that any property you buy is free of any charges or you will be liable to pay them and not the previous owner.

It is essential to confirm that any property you buy is free of any liens or encumbrances or you will be liable to pay any outstanding charges, as charges will be against the property and not against the previous owner. Your lawyer should check this for you. You should request a "Nota Simple" which is a summary of the property details and any charges against it.

UTILITIES

Often the bank that offers you a mortgage will insist that at least some regular bills go through the account and your utility bills are good candidates for this.

Electricity

Once you have bought your Spanish property, check all past bills have been paid and then sign a contract with the local electricity company to start from the day you move in. It's Iberdrola in Murcia, *www.iberdrola.es* or 901 202 020, unless you buy in Corvera or La Murta and then you'll contact Corvera Electrica 968 607 473.

You can usually register online or by phone rather than needing to visit a branch. You will need:

- ❑ Passport or residence card
- ❑ The contract and bills paid by the previous owner
- ❑ The reference number for your electricity supply (on a bill from the previous owner, if you have one)

You will receive a bill every two months. If it is based on an estimate then make sure you know how to read the meter to check you are not being overcharged.

Water

Water is controlled by the local municipality and charges can range from €50-300 to install water in your home in an urban area or up to €1,500 in rural areas. You may choose to have a water deposit in a rural area and have tanker loads of water delivered.

There is usually a quarterly charge for a minimum consumption, even if you don't use any water during the billing period. To transfer a water contract into your name, go to your local town hall with your passport (or residence card) and previous bills from the former owner. Non-residents will also need to give their foreign address.

In the North of the region Aqualia supply water
www.aqualia.es

For the rest of the region Aguas de Murcia is the supplier
www.emuasa.es.

MORTGAGE

This is the normal way to finance a property if you don't have the full amount of the purchase price. The mortgage market in Spain appears to be less sophisticated than in the UK with fewer options.

There are special products designed for non-resident borrowers and you should also consider getting a mortgage in your home country. A financial advisor will be able to help you.

Some notes:

- The mortgage will be filed at the Spanish Property Registry (*Registro de la Propiedad*). A non-registered mortgage is considered an ordinary loan.

- Mortgages must be formalised before a Public Notary.

- The property must be registered at the Property Registry with the name of the owners for whom the mortgage is given.

- Fixed and variable rate mortgages are available.

The mortgage market in Spain is less sophisticated than in the UK with fewer options - especially for foreign buyers.

Costs and Legal Fees

If you intend to mortgage a secondhand property the following costs apply:

- Valuation of the property.

- *Nota Simple* issued by the Spanish Property Registry, which shows the latest recorded details of any charges on the property.

- Bank mortgage opening fee paid when signing the deeds. This fee varies depending on the lending bank you deal with. Some banks do not charge this fee.

- Stamp duty (*Impuesto de Actos Jurídicos Documentados*) of 0.5%.

- Notary and Registry fees vary depending on the guaranteed capital of the mortgage.

- Insurance - the banks normally require the borrower to buy at least a fire insurance policy to protect its interest until the loan is repaid. The bank will try you to sell you insurance with the company they have an agreement with. It is your right to buy insurance with whomever you wish. The insurance fee must be paid at the moment of the deed signature.

The bank will try to sell you insurance with a company they have an agreement with but it almost always pays to shop around for this.

Once you have decided which mortgage suits you best, the lender will analyse your current income and basic credit history situation in order to qualify you for a maximum loan amount.

Buying Property in Murcia

The documents typically required by a bank are:

- Your *NIE*
- Your contract of employment
- Your last 3 payslips
- Your latest income tax return
- Your pre-agreement with the seller
- Proof that the property tax (*IBI*) on the house is paid up
- Details of other mortgages or loans that you may have
- All property titles, both in Spain and overseas
- Certificate from work authorities (*vida laboral*) showing your past work history
- Records of your current assets (bank/mutual fund statements etc.)
- Prenuptial agreements, marriage certificate or divorce papers, if any
- Nonresidents: a certificate of nonresidency - a form for this is available from the bank
- If self-employed: local tax on economic activities (*IAE*)
- If self-employed: records of your assets during the last two years
- If self-employed: VAT (*IVA*) tax you paid for the last quarter and last year

If the lender decides to give you the loan requested, he will issue an offer, which includes the loan conditions. Normally you will be given a term of 10 days to accept or reject this offer. The offer will contain: principal loaned, interests rates, fees, payment term and interest for delayed payment.

The mortgage shall be formalised by signing before the Notary of your choice though the bank will probably choose the Notary *they* prefer.

It is your right to examine the full contract with at least 3 working days notice. The parties must be present for the signing and the Notary shall make sure that the borrowers understand everything they are signing.

The borrowers should examine the mortgage conditions, especially when the mortgage interest is variable. The bank will keep a true copy of the deed to be filed before the court in case the borrower does not pay the mortgage.

Worked Costing Example

Here's an example to show how the costs might work out. Remember this is just an example and you need to have legal advice. Your lawyer will also be able to give you sample costings based on your own circumstances.

Jim and Mary found a villa in Fuente Álamo and negotiated a price of €250,000. The seller, Miguel, did not use an estate agent.

Jim and Mary signed a *contrato de arras*. The seller asked for a downpayment of €25,000.

Jim and Mary then went to a bank for a mortgage of €200,000. The bank offered them a variable-rate mortgage for Euribor+0.5% with no opening fee and no cancellation fee. Nice bank!

The bank requested the following documents from Miguel:

- A copy of his *DNI* (a national's equivalent of the *Tarjeta de Residencia* card that resident foreigners apply for)
- Receipts showing he was paid up on his property tax (*IBI*), building fees and mortgage

Once all of Jim and Mary's documents were presented it took one week for them to be pre-approved. It took another 2 weeks for the bank to get an appraisal (*tasacion*) done on the property and another 3 days for the bank to hear back from the appraiser.

The appraised value was €200,000 so the bank approved the loan. Jim and Mary went to the bank to sign the mortgage contract. They were also required to get property insurance (€100/year) and life insurance which came to €180/year.

They also had to *domiciliar* a few things in the bank account – in other words, the bank insists that some transactions occur regulary from the mortgage account. They called the gas and electric company to have automatic withdrawals done through this account. The bank then gave them an estimate of what the mortgage payments would be as well as a listing of the various fees (*provisión de fondos*) that they would need to pay. The *provisión de fondos* appeared as follows:

- **Lawyer's fee: €2000**
- **Downpayment: €2500** paid to the seller on signing *contrato de arras*
- **Appraisal: €300** due to the bank immediately
- **Deposit: €25000** due to the bank a week before the closing
- **Taxes: €19100** due to the bank a week before the closing
- **Notary fees: €1275** due to the bank a week before the closing
- **Property Registry: €640** due to the bank a week before the closing
- **Bank fees: €0** what a lovely bank!

Total: €73,315

Jim and Mary transferred €48,315 to the bank to pay the rest of what they owed (€73,315 minus the €25,000 to the seller for the contrato de arras) 1 week before the final signing.

1 week later they did the signing with the Notary and the seller and the bank. Miguel received the cheque from the bank and gave Jim and Mary the keys to the villa.

This is a very simple example. We assumed Miguel was resident in Spain, so no need to withhold the 5% tax for non-residents. Also we assumed Miguel didn't have a mortgage in our calculations, which whilst associated costs would be paid by Miguel, the overall calculations would look a little more complex. Also, there wasn't an estate agent involved in the transaction.

In total the minimum costs of buying this property were about 30% of the property price assuming an 80% mortgage was available. If you estimate around 30% of the price of the property to cover fees and your own deposit then you should be okay. Costs can generally be estimated at around 10-15%.

Of course, if you don't need a mortgage then the solicitor and notary fees will be lower, and there won't be a bank fee.

BUDGET CALCULATOR
(Make a Copy & Fill It In)

Property Price _____

Transfer Tax (at 7% on declared value) _____

Legal Document Tax (at 1% on declared value) _____

VAT – IVA (approx 7% on declared value) _____

Estate Agent's Fee (upto 25%) _____

Agent's Viewing Fee _____

Travel (Flights/Car) _____

Notary Fee (approx €500) _____

Stamp Duty – New Properties (0.5% on declared value) _____

Deed Registration Fee (upto €500) _____

Maintenance Charges _____

TOTAL COST _____

Budgeting is a complicated matter and there are many variables in the calculations. Double check your sums to avoid nasty surprises and ask your lawyer for a sanity check.

PURCHASING A NEW BUILD/OFF PLAN PROPERTY

Initial Phase

When buying an unfinished (new build or off plan) property in Spain, the developer is legally required to provide you with the following information:

- ❑ Company details of the Developer registered at the Spanish Company Registry (Registro Mercantil), its trading name and address.
- ❑ Location information for the development and your unit.
- ❑ Building specifications and description of the electricity, water, gas and heating networks and fire protection measures.
- ❑ Dimensions and specification of the fixtures and fittings. This information is contained in the memoria de calidades.
- ❑ Property description and details of the common areas and community services.
- ❑ Price of the property and community services and terms of payment.

Keep in mind that anything the developer publishes must be performed, as the information the developer supplies has the power of a legal contract.

Keep all documents, make print outs of webpages, save all emails.

Deposit & Staged Payments

You normally have to reserve your property while it is being built - and to do this you will be required to make a deposit and advance staged payments. You will usually sign a private contract with the seller and put down a non-returnable deposit (about 10% of the total property price).

The private contract should contain the following provisions:

- ❑ Seller and buyer identification.
- ❑ Seller and buyer legal capacity to make a contract.
- ❑ Description of the property; details of common areas, community services, and its location.
- ❑ The selling price and taxes levied on the property to be paid.
- ❑ That in case of dispute, both parties agree to submit to the exclusive competence of the Spanish courts in the location of the property.
- ❑ Signature of the parties to the purchase contract.
- ❑ Payment terms while the unit is under construction, up to its completion.
- ❑ Bank account details where advanced payments are to be paid in.
- ❑ Reference to the penalties to be applied either in case the buyer does not complete the payment terms agreed, or the seller does not provide the property as promised.

To reserve your property you will be required to make a non-returnable deposit (usually about 10% of the property price) and advance staged payments.

- Possession Date: the date when the buyer will take possession of the house. The contract shall also contain the penalty applicable in case the developer does not complete the construction of the property on time.
- Plan of the property and its description and specifications (memoria de calidades).

You will need to open a bank account to make the staged payments.

Your staged payments should be protected by an insurance policy while the property is being built.

Together with the private contract, the developer must provide you the following documentation:

- Description of the property and the building where it is located, the common areas and community services.
- Plans of the property and its location.
- Construction details: electric wire, fire protection measures...
- Reference to the materials used in the construction of the property.
- Details of registration of the building in the Property Registry (Registro de la Propiedad), or mention to the non-registration of it.
- Copy of the building permit

This is not the final contract.

If you have to pay the full purchase price before the property has been completed, by law, you must have the benefit of a bank guarantee to ensure that if the developer goes bankrupt before the completion of the building work that you do not lose your money. In some parts of Spain developers try to ignore this legal requirement.

You also need to make sure that the property specification is agreed in detail with the builder and that the property will be delivered to you complete with the necessary licence to occupy it as a home.

Completion

When the property is completed you will sign a sales contract (*contrato de Escritura de Compra-venta*) before a Spanish Notary. This shall contain the mortgage details and the specifics including amount, rate and term, where applicable. Not until this is signed will you own the property.

The purchase deed must be registered with the Spanish Property Registry (*Registro de la Propiedad*). Once that is done the title deed (*Escritura Pública de Compra-Venta*) fully assures your title: the registered contract makes you the owner of the property.

The registration of the house is also important for tax purposes as real estate tax (IBI) must be paid yearly, otherwise you could be fined.

If you cannot be present to sign the contract, you can make a power of attorney allowing another person to

The Notary is the public official who makes the contract legal. He keeps the original document in his files in case any problem could arise later. Note that the notary does not certify that all statements are true, only that the parties have sworn to them!

Buying Property in Murcia

sign it for you, if necessary. You should receive the keys of your property upon signature of the contract in the presence of the Notary. Easy!

Taxes and Fees

In order to pay your taxes (and therefore to buy a property) you will need a Spanish tax identification number – a NIE if you are not Spanish and a NIF of you are. For purchasing a new property the following taxes apply:

- Value Added Tax - (*IVA*) 7% of the total price. It must be paid as the sale is a business operation between a developer and a private individual.
- Stamp Duty - (*Impuesto de Actos Jurídicos Documentados*) 0.5% Must be paid upon signing the Contrato de Escritura de Compra-venta) at the notary office.

The following fees, subject to IVA, shall also be paid:

- Notary (*Notario*): You must pay the notary fees when you sign the deed. These are fixed on an official scale and will vary depending on the size of the property.
- Property Pegistry (*Registro de la Propiedad*): You must pay the registration of the deed at the Spanish Property Registry in order for the property to be transferred to you. Before going to the registry you should have paid the corresponding taxes and the receipts must be given to the Registrar. Your lawyer will tell you how much these are.

Value Added Tax (IVA) must be paid on the purchase of new properties as a business transaction is taking place between you and a business.

Moving to Spain - What Do You Do About Tax?

For those readers planning on moving to Spain permanently there will be a list of things you need to sort out and one of them is tax planning. If you are one of these people, do you know what your tax liabilities will be in Spain and how and where you will pay your tax? The tax year in Spain runs from 1st January to 31st December, different from the UK which is 6th April to 5th April. This can be of some advantage if you plan ahead before leaving for Spain.

The law dictates that you will become a tax resident in Spain if you spend more that 183 days of the tax year in Spain. The days do not have to be consecutive and you become liable whether or not you formally register as a resident of Spain.

You could leave the UK near the end of a tax year, say 30th March, and spend time elsewhere so that your total days in Spain for that year are less than the 183 days. In this way you can delay becoming a tax resident until the following year assuming you then spend 183 days or more in Spain. The 183 day rule is not the only provision in determining tax resident status. If you don't spend 183 days in Spain in a calendar year you can still become a tax resident if your "centre of vital interests" is in Spain i.e. the base of your economic or professional activities is in Spain; or if your spouse lives in Spain and you are not legally separated you are presumed Spanish resident, unless proven otherwise.

Fiscal identity number

You will need a fiscal identity number (NIE - *número de identificación extranjero*). This identifies you to the Spanish tax authority (*'Hacienda'*) when paying your taxes. Your Spanish lawyer, accountant or *gestor* (an intermediary between you and the authorities) may secure one for you, particularly if you buy a property in Spain, so you may already have one. An NIE can be obtained from the local provincial Foreigners' Office (*la Oficina de Extranjeros*), or the nearest National Police Station (*Comisaria de Policia*) that has a foreigner's department.

You will need a photocopy of the relevant identification page of your passport, which contains your photograph, proof of address in the UK and Spain (if you do not have a Spanish address your solicitor or estate agent can be used). You also need to supply written justification of why you require an NIE, which can be supplied by your lawyer, estate agent or bank manager. You also need to obtain a residence certificate from the Foreigners' Office (in place of the old-style residencia) if you want to remain in Spain.

Tax liabilities

Spanish tax residents are liable for tax on their worldwide assets, which includes anything they may still have in the UK.

Income tax – Income is split into general income (renta general) and savings income (renta del ahorro). General income is taxed at progressive scale rates. There are four tax bands which range from 24% to 43%. Anything not categorised as 'savings income' is included here such as salary, pension and rental income. Savings income is taxed at a fixed rate of 18% and includes interest and dividends, income from a purchased annuity and capital gains. Remember that this is tax on your worldwide income, although any tax paid in the UK can be credited against the Spanish liability under the terms of the double tax treaty.

Wealth tax - Spanish wealth tax is based on your assets held at 31st December each year. There are deductions of €108,182 (general) and €150,253 (own home). Tax rates vary between 0.2% for assets up to €167,129 and 2.5% for assets valued at €10,695,996 and over.

Succession tax – This tax on inheritances and gifts is paid by the beneficiary and not the estate as is the case in the UK. It is paid if the beneficiary is a resident of Spain or the asset concerned is located in Spain. Succession tax rates range from 7.65% on assets valued at €7,993 or less, to 34% on assets of €797,555 and over. There are various allowances depending on the beneficiary's relationship with the deceased. It is worth noting that although there is no blanket exemption for inheritances between spouses in Spain as there is in the UK, Spain is slowly reducing succession tax between spouses and in the direct line. In Valencia, Alicante and Castellon, for example, the inheritance tax rate is now less than 1% between resident spouses and direct line relatives. So if you have not yet decided which area in Spain to move to it may be beneficial researching the rules for the different regions.

It is important to note that if you remain a UK domiciled person while living in Spain you will still be liable for UK inheritance tax on your worldwide assets, which will include Spanish assets, as well as being liable for Spanish succession tax. Although there is no Spain/UK double tax treaty for inheritance taxes, any tax paid in Spain can be deducted from the UK tax due on the same asset and vice-versa.

Tax Returns

Tax returns relating to the income and capital gains made during the year to 31st December have to be made in May or June of the following year. So if you move to Spain during the first half of 2008 you will not have to make your first return until May/June 2009. If your tax affairs are straightforward and your total income is less than €22,000 you do not have to submit a tax return provided certain conditions are met, but these are not likely to apply to most expatriates, and in many cases people would be entitled to a tax refund if they filled in a Spanish tax return.

Organising tax returns and paying tax is not something that most people do with enthusiasm. Nevertheless, it is the law and when relocating to Spain it is good to know what to expect tax-wise so that you are not taken by surprise or fall foul of the law. As daunting as it may feel to some, it does not have to be difficult. A professional tax adviser can help with your tax planning and advise you on how you can legitimately mitigate your tax liabilities both in Spain and the UK, even if in the future you decide to return to the UK to live.

Bill Blevins
Managing Director of Blevins Franks, who offer financial advice for expats.
www.blevinsfranksinternational.com
UK: Jane Hayward ☎020 7015 2126 *jane.hayward@blevinsfranks.com*
Murcia: Neil Jenkins ☎965 705 502 *neil.jenkins@blevinsfranks.com*
www.blevinsfranks.com

Check List

- **Building Plots** - when you are planning to buy a property within an urbanisation zone in Spain, you should first check the Partial Plan (*Plan Parcial*). It is the plan of building plots, which must be approved by the town-planning department of the Town Hall. This plan assures that your urbanisation is legal and that there are no other developments planned nearby that could affect your new property.

- **The Coastal Law** - If your property is going to be built near the beach then make sure that your property will comply with The Spanish Coastal Law (*Ley de Costas*) of 1988. The builder should have an authorisation from the Coast department, which provides that the authorities must restrict building within 100 metres of the beach and establishes a zone of influence (*zona de influencia*) up to one kilometre inland.

- The builder must have obtained the building licence (*licencia de obra*) issued by the Town Hall, which allows him to build the house.

- The certificate of the building completion (*certificado de fin de obra*) is issued by the architect once the building is complete. The developer needs it in order to get the certificate of occupancy.

- The developer must provide you with the certificate of occupancy, which is issued by the *Ayuntamiento*. This administrative document permits you to inhabit your new dwelling.

Before you can legally live in your new home you must obtain a certificate of occupancy from the developer which is issued by the Ayuntamiento.

Snagging

Once you receive your keys you should check your house in order to detect whether there are any defects.

For houses with applications for building licenses issued before May of 2000, the guarantee periods are:
- 6 months from the date the deed was signed for defective construction, which has no effect on the building's final purpose.
- 10 years from the date of completion of the works for defective construction of the essential parts of a building.
- 15 years for the cases in which the contractor had not complied with the terms of the contract.

For houses with applications for building licences issued after May 2000, the guarantee periods are:
- 1 year for defective construction, which has an adverse effect on the finish of the house such as electricity installations, painting etc. In this case, the builder is responsible for all property damages.
- 3 years for defective construction, which has an adverse effect on the habitability conditions such as humidity. In this case the other agents involved in the construction of the building are liable for the property damages.
- 10 years for defective construction, which has an adverse effect on the building structure.

Spanish law provides a time limit of 2 years to claim for construction defects from the date on which the defect was apparent and known to the proprietor, provided that the defect arose during the guarantee period described above.

Guaranteed Rental Schemes - The Lowdown

Rental guarantee schemes have increased in popularity over the past few years as developers continue to create new incentives to attract buyers. On paper they look very good; the developer undertakes to find you tenants and guarantees all payments while all you need to do is hand over the keys for the specified number of years. This is essentially what happens. However, you will need to consider the price you pay for this privilege and bear in mind the following factors:

- The developers will have to re-coup the cost of their generous offer, namely by including it in your purchase price. Typically many will offer you a gross rental guarantee of say, 5% while the purchase price is quietly raised by 15% - more than covering the guaranteed rental. Therefore you will essentially be paid back with your own money.
- Many developers are not interested in obtaining a maximum rental value for your property as they have already more than recouped their money with the sale. You, the owner, might find that when the guarantee period ends, you are stuck with the existing low rental payments, which are difficult to increase, while some developers don't bother renting units out at all.
- At the end of the rental guarantee period, you may find that your property is one of many in a glut of properties newly up for rental. Yours may take time to rent or be difficult to shift.
- If you are confident you can rent the property out yourself and you have calculated the value of the rental guarantee offer, you may need to ask for this as a discount on the purchase price up front.

However, not all developers are the same and it would be unfair to brand them all as guilty of a cheeky scam. In fact, there are many genuine companies who work ethically, serving to enhance investor confidence and continue to provide an excellent product. Look out for the good signs when picking your property. A company offering a good guaranteed rental agreement will:

- Not overprice your property by huge percentages to more than cover your rental guarantee. However you will need to bear in mind they will not be giving anything away either.
- The guaranteed rental agreement is made on the basis of signed contracts with national and international tour operators. Travel agencies pre-book blocks of the year and supply bank guarantees.

❑ Keep your property permanently occupied with genuine rentals, usually linked with tour operators and holiday lets within a good niche market that will continue to feed your investment.

The best advice for all investors is to make seven simple checks to be sure your developer is offering a genuine deal:

1. Add up the items making up the price of the terms offered in the guarantee offer, including legal fees, stamp duty and deduct this from the asking price. This will give you the actual price of the property, which you can then compare with other similar options. This can become a clever bargaining tool.

2. Study the rental market in the area and work out if your property stands a good chance of rental. On what basis are the developers guaranteeing to rent out your property and will you be able to do so when the guaranteed rental period is over?

3. What is the infrastructure like around your property? Will it be adequate for the rental market proposed?

4. Make sure your property is located within an established, or preferably an up-and-coming area, which is becoming popular. In this way your property will be commercially viable and a good investment. It must be continually in demand as a holiday home to fetch a fair price.

5. Is the developer obliging you to accept their furniture pack as part of the deal? If so, how much is this really costing you and is it a fair price?

6. Be aware that gross guarantees do not include costs such as service charges, management fees and ground rent, while net guarantees do.

7. Add up the total income from the rental guarantee and make the comparison with a comparable property without a guaranteed rental agreement. If the price difference is greater than the net guarantee, then ask for a discount.

So the name of the game is be vigilant and don't allow a salesman to talk you into a deal that is not worth the paper it is written on.

IPIN (International Property Investment Network) operated by www.propertyshowrooms.com is a global collaboration of agents, developers and investment specialists bringing its members only the most highly qualified and niche property investment opportunities.

PURCHASING A SECOND-HAND/RESALE PROPERTY

Initial Phase

Initially ask for a *Nota Simple* from the Property Registry, in order to obtain the full details of the owner and the exact size of the property. You can also check whether the property is free of charges or is otherwise subject to mortgages, restrictions on use, court orders for seizure, etc. Your estate agent should be able to get this for you.

If there's a mortgage on the property then make sure that the seller can prove that the payments are up to date; otherwise the bank could seize the property.

Check if the house is already rented out as Spanish rental law protects the tenants. To do this, make sure that the purchasing contract states that the house is not rented out.

If you are buying an apartment it is advisable to ask the President or Administrator of the Community of Property Owners whether the monthly community fees are paid or not, since the buyer would need to pay any outstanding fees. In any case the seller must provide you with a certificate to specify that the fee payments are up to date.

If you like the look of a property then the first thing to do is to request a Nota Simple from the Property Registry.

Check that the municipal real estate tax (*IBI - Impuesto sobre Bienes Inmuebles*) is paid, otherwise you, as the new owner, will need to pay the back tax and penalties.

If the seller is a Company then you will need their tax identification code (*CIF-Código de Identificación Fiscal*) from the Spanish Company Register. If the seller is an estate agent then they must provide you with their registration number for the estate agent's professional association.

Make sure all taxes are paid on a property you're purchasing or else you could be hit with the previous owner's bill.

The Community of Property Owners

If you have bought an apartment or villa in a building complex it will be subject to the Spanish Law of Horizontal Division (*Ley de Propiedad Horizontal*). This law is applicable whether you are resident or not.

According to this law every apartment or villa-owner has the co-ownership of the common elements of the building complex (stairs, lifts, façades, swimming pool, cleaning services, drains, supply of water, electric wires etc), together with the rest of owners of the block.

All property owners of the block form the Community of Property Owners (*Comunidad de Propietarios*). They are responsible for their individual parts and common areas of the block. They shall maintain the common elements of the building. All of them participate in the expenses of the community on a pro-rata basis. Only those who buy an individual property standing on its own land will not have to join a community of property owners.

Every apartment of the block has a share (*cuota de participación*) in the common property, usually proportionate to the size of the owner's property. Therefore the owner of a large flat will have a larger share in the common property, this share determines the community charges and voting rights of the homeowner.

The urbanisations are ruled by a different law (as they share elements with the outside world such as street lighting, refuse collection, roads), however, the Spanish Law of Horizontal Division may also be applied to them provided that they meet some specific requirements.

It is advisable to check at the Spanish Property Registry (*Registro de la Propiedad*) the physical description of your apartment and the building that is attached to, in this way you will find out your property size and your common-area share.

The Spanish Property Registry may also provide you with the rules about the use of the common facilities, general management and maintenance, which take part of the Statutes of the Community of

Owners. The statutes and the decisions taken at previous meetings will bind every new owner automatically.

You should also make sure the seller is up to date with his payments, otherwise the unpaid back community fees could be charged to the new owner. If you are purchasing in a new development the rules of the Community must be explained to you and approved by you.

Most communities have a wide set of rules which govern the property owners rights and standards of behaviour expected from the persons who reside on the complex. The Statutes of the community may only be modified by unanimous vote of the community owners, both present and by proxy. If Statutes need changing they are discussed at the annual general meeting.

If any member of the community violates the statutes the community members can vote to ask the court to issue an injunction, which will forbid him from entering his property for a period of up to 2 years.

Besides the Statutes, the owners may establish internal rules, setting out standards of behaviour for the community members and use of the common services. The owners are also obliged to comply with these rules, which may be modified by a simple majority vote.

Every community owner can make repairs in their own property (flat, attached house, etc) under the following conditions:

- Previous notice to the Community owners.
- If the general structure and façade of the building is not modified.
- Avoid causing any damage to the rights of other community owners.

The community owners are obliged to adhere to the following:

- They must let work be carried out in their own flat when it is necessary for proper maintenance of the building or the installation of new services. For that purpose, they shall permit workmen to enter their property. Should any damage arise as a result of these works, the community must pay an indemnity.

- They must respect the indivisible parts of the complex where the property is located: care of drains, electric wiring and any other installations, which serve other owners, they must also care for their own installations.
- Maintain their property in good condition so that it does not cause any damage to the other owners. When causing damages to other owners, an indemnity shall be paid.
- They shall contribute, according to their community share, to the maintenance costs of the complex.
- On selling the property the seller should provide a certificate showing either that he or she has no pending debts with the community, or those community debts which are still pending of payment.
- The secretary of the community must be informed about the address of the owners in Spain, in order to send them those notifications relating to the community owners. If it is been impossible to send the notifications to the referred address, this will be placed in a visible place in the community complex.
- The Secretary of the Community shall be informed of the sale of the property; otherwise the seller will also be liable, together with the new owner, for the community debts of the property sold.

Rights of the property owners

- You have the right to attend the annual general meeting as well as any extraordinary meetings of the community.
- You are also entitled to be informed in advance of the dates and the order of business of any meeting called. If you are not correctly informed, you can protest and even have the results of the meeting annulled by a court.
- At the meeting you have the right to voice your opinion, the right to vote and to present motions for the vote of the other members.
- You may be elected president, the vice-president or the secretary of the community.
- You may check the documentation and records of the community.

The community members shall meet at least once a year:

- ❏ To elect the President and the Administrator.
- ❏ To propose the budget for the coming year as well as other matters, such as the accounts and expenditures of the previous year.
- ❏ To approve the Statutes of the Community and determine the internal rules.
- ❏ To check other business arising for the better management of the community, etc...

The President shall give notice of the meeting to the community members in advance. The meeting shall be presided over by the president. Most of decisions are taken by majority vote of the community members.

An Arras Agreement (Contrato de Arras) enables you to secure your chosen house. When you sign this agreement you put down a deposit which you will lose if you don't complete the sale on the date stated. The vendor is required to give you double the amount deposited if he or she does not honour the contract within the stated timeframe.

Payment & Completion

Once you've decided upon a property (at the same time as making mortgage arrangements) get the paperwork in order and have detailed surveys carried out.

You may also want to "secure" the house at this stage. This is called an Arras Agreement (*Contrato de Arras*). When you sign this agreement you are putting-down a deposit to secure the property. You will lose this deposit if you don't complete the sale on the date stated but the vendor shall give you double the amount deposited if he or she does not honour the contract within the stated date. It is advisable to put the deposit into a blocked bonded escrow account.

You will sign a sales contract (*contrato de Escritura de Compra-venta*) before a Spanish Notary. This shall contain the mortgage details and the specifics including amount, rate and term, where applicable. The contract must accurately describe the property you are buying, fully identify the seller and buyer, and state that the property is free of charges. Not until this is signed will you own the property.

The purchase deed must be registered with the Spanish Property Registry (*Registro de la Propiedad*). Once that is done the title deed (*Escritura Pública de Compra-Venta*) fully assures your title: the registered contract makes you the owner of the property.

The registration of the house is also important for tax purposes as real estate tax (*IBI*) must be paid yearly, otherwise you could be fined.

If you cannot be present to sign the contract, you can make a power of attorney allowing another person to sign it for you, if necessary. You should receive the keys to your property upon signature of the contract in the presence of the Notary.

Taxes and Fees

In order to pay these taxes (and therefore to buy a property) you will need a Spanish tax identification number – a NIE if you are not Spanish and a NIF of you are. Second hand properties incur the following taxes and fees:

- ❏ The transfer tax (*Impuesto de Transmisiones Patrimoniales - ITP*) The purchaser must pay this upon signature of the sales contract. Its value is 6 % of the purchasing price, as indicated in the sales contract. If the purchasing price declared is much lower than the approximate market value the Tax inspectors may decide that the purchasing price is too low and you may receive penalties. Your Lawyer can help you in this matter by asking the tax office what is the market value of the property that you are willing to buy.

If you cannot be present to sign the contract then you can make a power of attorney allowing another person to sign it for you.

- Capital Gains Tax on Land (*Plusvalía*): This is the tax on the increase in the value of the property since the last sale. Although it must be paid by the seller, often both parties agree that the buyer will pay it.

The following fees, subject to VAT, shall also be paid:

- Notary (*Notario*): You must pay the notary fees when you sign the deed. These are fixed on an official scale and will vary depending on the size of the property.
- Property Pegistry (*Registro de la Propiedad*): You must pay the registration of the deed at the Spanish Property Registry in order for the property to be transferred to you. Before going to the registry you should have paid the corresponding taxes, and the receipts must be given to the Registrar. Your lawyer will tell you how much these are.

You must pay for the Registro de la Propiedad at the Spanish Property Registry in order for ownership of the property to be transferred to you.

Check List

- **Building Plots** - when you are planning to buy a property within an urbanisation zone in Spain you should first check the Partial Plan (*Plan Parcial*). It is the plan of building plots, which must be approved by the town-planning department of the Town Hall. This plan assures that your urbanisation is legal and that there are no other developments planned nearby that could affect your property.

- **The Coastal Law** - If your property is near the beach, make sure that your property complies with The Spanish Coastal Law (*Ley de Costas*) of 1988.

- Check that the building licence (*licencia de obra*) issued by the Town Hall is in order.

- Check that the certificate of building completion (*certificado de fin de obra*) is in order. The developer needs it in order to get the certificate of occupancy.

- Check that the certificate of occupancy, which is issued by the Town Hall (*Ayuntamiento*) is in order.

The term of guarantee for possible construction defects for new houses also applies to resale properties.

Snagging

Once you receive your keys you should check your house is in order to detect whether there are any defects. The term of guarantee for possible construction defects for new houses is also applicable to resales.

TOWNHOUSES, FINCAS AND RURAL PROPERTIES

The building rules in Murcia change depending upon which municipality you happen to buy in. For example the rules in Fuente Álamo are different to Álhama de Murcia. Often an estate agent will have properties in multiple municipalities so you must take care to know what the rules for each are. Your estate agent may not know the differences either and assume blanket rules.

If you are looking at a major renovation project then before deciding to buy ensure that you will be able to rebuild by running your own check using your gestor, abogado and architect. Never trust the word of the estate agent or vendor in these matters.

As for the rest of the process - the guidelines for second-hand homes apply here too. See the previous section - Purchasing a Second-Hand/Resale Property, on page 174. However, other considerations must be taken. Ownership issues, due to the inheritance laws in Spain, mean that properties may or may not be registered and boundaries may be an issue.

If you are looking at a major renovation project then check that you will be able to get permission to rebuild before deciding to buy. Never trust the word of the estate agent or vendor in these matters.

Buying a Property Which Does Not Have a Registered Title Deed

These cases often occur in country houses either because the former owners avoided paying transfer taxes and fees, because the owners of the property are family members whose family never registered the title, or because the original owner had died without registering the property.

Alternatively the property of your dreams may already be registered in the name of a person who no longer claims it because he sold it to someone on a private contract and this person never registered the sale!

If you are willing to buy a property which does not have a public title deed (*escritura pública de compra-venta*) then you may establish the title through a process called *Expediente de Dominio*.

This is a long and complex process, which requires court action and involves publication of your claim in the National Official Gazette. You also file a certificate at the Spanish Property Registry (*Registro de la Propiedad*) and the Catastro office (*Oficina del Catastro*) describing the state of the property and that it is not legally registered. The Catastro Office keeps records of each plot's description and its assessed value for tax purposes. The court's decision shall determine the title of your property.

You may establish the public title deed (escritura pública de compra-venta) through a complex process called Expediente de Dominio.

These are only general guidelines and not definitive statements of the law, all questions about the law's applications to individual cases should be directed to a Spanish Lawyer experienced in these types of cases.

Buying From a Non-Resident

If you are buying a property in Spain from a non-resident property owner then be aware that you should deposit 5% of the purchase price against any tax due from the seller. The form is available from Spanish Tax offices (*Oficinas de Hacienda*) for this purpose and your Lawyer should be able to arrange this for you.

If the purchase price declared is much lower than the approximate market value the tax inspectors could feel that the purchase price is too low and you may receive heavy penalties, so get good legal advice.

If the purchase price declared is much lower than the approximate market value you may be fined.

BUILDING A HOUSE

Initial Phase

If you are buying land to have a house built in Spain then you should first find out whether the land is located in an area where building is allowed.

Land in Spain is classified as follows:

- Land for development (*Suelo Urbano*).
- Green zones (*Zonas verdes*) where no building can take place.
- Rural areas (*Suelo Rústico*) where no construction is permitted.

Other details also come into play such as rules limiting building size in relation to plot size. Each municipality will have different rules so you must get local professional advice.

The classification of the land is also important in order to get a mortgage. For example to get a mortgage on a plot of land where building is not allowed (*Suelo Rústico*) the maximum mortgage amount you can raise will be 50% of the value and the maximum term will be 12 years.

Check at the Property Registry whether the land you want to buy is free of charges.

If your land is in the countryside you should check at the Town Hall (*Ayuntamiento*) where the property is registered to see whether there are any impediments. For example a path may cross your land and you can't build your house as the path would be cut.

Buying Property in Murcia

Whether you design the house yourself or use existing models you will need the services of an architect to get your building permit.

You should also inspect the Town Plan and the *plan parcial* (if you are buying a plot located within an urbanisation), in order to know the developments planned for the area where your land is located (roads, water supply, airports etc.) and if the urbanistion is registered and legal.

Payment & Completion

Once you have determined that you can buy the land and build your house you will sign a sales contract (*contrato de Escritura de Compra-venta*) before a Spanish Notary. This shall contain the mortgage details and the specifics including amount, rate and term, where applicable. The contract must accurately describe the plot you are buying, fully identify the seller and buyer, and state that the plot is free of charges. Not until this is signed will you own the plot.

You can design your house yourself or get models of houses. You will need the services of an architect as his drawings are needed to get your building permit.

You also need to find a reliable builder whom you will sign a contract with. Your Spanish lawyer must check this contract. It shall state the payment terms and completion date with penalty clauses for late completion etc.

A clerk of works (*aparejador*) will supervise the building and ensure that it complies with the construction standards. He will issue the architect's certificates to obtain the certificate of building completion (*certificado de fin de obra*) and certificate of occupancy.

Then you must register the house at the Spanish Property Registry, as your deeds contain only the plot registration. You should make a declaration of new work (*declaración de obra nueva*) in order that your house appears in the deed. The building permit, the certificate of building completion and the certificate of occupancy will be also required.

If you are non-resident then you will also need to present a bank certificate to show that you have imported the money from abroad and are not using black money earned in Spain.

Other Options
Wooden Houses

Wooden houses require planning permission in Murcia. Installing a wooden house without permission will result in a fine, proportional to the size of the house and dependent upon its location. You may also receive a demolition order.

Interhouse - Poligono Industrial Lorqui
☎ 968 690035

Antonio Moreno - Murcia
☎ 629 628716

Caravans

There is no specific law, *yet*, in Murcia that prevents you from parking a caravan on any piece of land that you own. This is the loophole that many Brits have to use (once they've been sold a dodgy piece of land by a dishonest estate agent) in order to live there and remain within the law.

Terramueble - Cesigres
CasasMalu - near Fuente Álamo
www.casasmalu.com
☎ 610 444432

Viewing and Due Diligence

VIEWING

Never buy in Spain without first viewing the property.

Make sure before you even start looking that you have an idea of what you want. What will you use your property for, how many rooms do you need, how much land, how often will you stay there?

Most often things go wrong when there aren't strong criteria for selection in place.

Draw up a wishlist and give this to your agents. This should mean that when you go to view they will only be showing you what you want and can afford - if they're not – stop viewing with them!

Make sure you have strong criteria in place before you start your property search.

PITFALLS

As with estate agents the world over, their job is to sell you a house, and they're generally good at it. You must take care that you keep your criteria in mind at all times and not get carried away with the enthusiasm of the seller.

Private sales can suffer from confusion (sometimes intentional!) and family in-fighting. Always use an abogado and let them do the "negotiating"!

Buying from developers has a myriad of chances of it all going wrong, as you're only initially buying an idea! Read the small print, speak to other people and be careful!

WHAT TO LOOK FOR

There are so many things to consider when viewing a property and often the most important questions are forgotten. Ensure you ask the relevant questions by taking our handy viewing checklist with you on your viewing.

There are a few general rules when viewing a property, especially older houses, which are detailed here:

- ❑ Does the property need updating? If so, how much will this cost?
- ❑ Is the property in a conservation area or a listed building and could this restrict any future alterations?
- ❑ Are the rooms big enough for your needs - furniture etc?
- ❑ What is included in the sale? Land, garage, furniture, fittings, etc.
- ❑ Are the views good enough?
- ❑ Why are they selling up or moving?
- ❑ Does the house have heating and air conditioning?
- ❑ How is the water (assuming it has water) heated?
- ❑ Has the property been altered in any way and if so are the relevant planning permissions available to inspect?

Read the small print, speak to other people and be careful!

There is a lot to consider when viewing a property so use a checklist to make sure you don't miss something important.

- ❏ Is there any sign of subsidence (e.g. major cracks in the walls or the doors sticking)?
- ❏ Is there any root damage to foundations from any big trees nearby?
- ❏ Is there a smell of damp or any other sign such as the walls feeling damp, the paint bubbling, watermarks or mould? We know it's generally sunny but it *does* rain here too!
- ❏ Has a room been recently redecorated and, if so, why? A problem might be lurking underneath that fresh paint and filler.
- ❏ Is there woodworm indicated by holes in beams and frames?
- ❏ How much storage space is there?
- ❏ Are there sufficient power points and how old (unsafe) do they look?
- ❏ Are there nearby railway lines, motorways or overhead flight paths?
- ❏ Does the community and local area feel friendly and safe?
- ❏ Is the aspect of the house right for you? Does it get enough light and is it overlooked?
- ❏ What are the actual boundaries and who owns what? Shared access to a well for example.
- ❏ Is the property well maintained?
- ❏ How old is the property?

- ❑ How big is the garden/plot you are buying?
- ❑ Are nearby properties in good condition?
- ❑ How good or close-by is reliable public transport?
- ❑ Are the local schools good?
- ❑ Are there any known plans for development in the area that could negatively or positively affect future value?
- ❑ What are the local amenities such as shops, hospitals, leisure facilities etc. like?
- ❑ What are crime levels like in the area?
- ❑ What are the neighbours like? Are they noisy or nosey?
- ❑ Has there ever been a dispute with the neighbours (or anyone living nearby)?

Check for planned developments that could negatively or positively affect the value of your home.

VIEWING CHECKLIST

Viewing Checklist
(Make A Copy For Each Property You View.
Remember To Take Photos & GPS Coordinates)

Property

- ❑ Price _____
- ❑ Bedrooms _____
- ❑ Area (internal) _____
- ❑ Area (land) _____
- ❑ Gas?
- ❑ Electricity?
- ❑ Water?

Location

- ❑ Rural
- ❑ Coast
- ❑ Mountain
- ❑ Golf

Access

- ❑ Poor
- ❑ Fair
- ❑ Good

Notes (pros/cons etc):

Notes
- Investment
- Rental
- Holidays
- For Family
- To Live

Additional Notes

RENTING BEFORE BUYING

Many people advise that before you decide to buy a property in Murcia you should rent a house in a location close to your chosen destination. This way you'll get a much better idea if the location will be right for you. Also, if at all possible, don't sell up in your home country but rent that house out.

You'll often find that the rental prices in Spain are much lower than the income you could get from renting your home in the UK, leaving you with some positive cashflow to help finance your plans.

The amount of rent is agreed between both parties. Normally rent is paid 7 days before the end of the month. On no account must the landlord ask for more than 1 month rent to be paid in advance. Payments should be made as stated in the contract.

Rent out your existing home to cover your rental costs in Murcia.

You should receive a written receipt showing that the rent has been paid, unless you pay through bank transfer where your receipt will be proof of payment. Make sure you get these receipts or any proof of payment as these constitute an implicit contract.

During the first 5 years rent will be increased or reduced according to the consumer price (inflation) index (*Índice de precios al Consumo - IPC*). After that period, rent will increase according to what both parties agreed when signing the contract.

Tenants must pay gas, electricity and telephone bills, unless otherwise agreed.

Tenants may be required to sign an inventory of the property contents (furnishing, fixtures and fittings) and the state of them. It is important to check this carefully, as every item outlined on the list shall be returned when you move out – otherwise you might lose your deposit.

The landlord must make all necessary repairs to keep the property in a fit and habitable condition however the landlord is not responsible for repairing any damage caused by the tenant.

It is a good idea to seek legal advice before agreeing to rent a property.

Urgent maintenance repairs may be undertaken by the tenant in order to avoid serious and immediate damage to the property. Reasonable repair costs will be returned to the tenant.

The landlord must give the tenant three-month's notice of the landlord's intent to undertake repairs relating to health, hygiene and comfort in the property. In this case the tenant may end the rental contract within 1 month of the notice. If the tenant decides to stay, he may get a reduced rental rate in relation to the rooms that cannot be used because of the repairs.

As usual, these are just general guidelines and you are strongly advised to seek legal advice.

If the landlord wishes to sell an occupied property during the life of the rental contract then the tenant has the right of pre-emption (*derecho de tanteo*), which means that he gets priority as a prospective purchaser above other purchasers.

So, the landlord must first offer the property to the tenant who will have 30 days to reply. If the landlord does not make this offer, or the property is sold at a lower price than the offered one, the tenant could, within one month following completion, have the sale annulled and purchase the property for the price declared in the sales document.

No pre-emption right can be applied when the rented house is sold along with other properties that form part of the same building, for example, an apartment block.

If you buy an occupied property then you acquire the rights and obligations of the vendor, and therefore, not until a 5-year validity period of the rental contract has been completed, may the rental be terminated.

If the landlord wants to sell an occupied property during the life of the rental contract then you, as the tenant, get priority as a prospective buyer.

The landlord may terminate the rental contract if the tenant:

- Does not pay the rent or deposit.
- Rents the property to a third party without the landlord's consent.
- Deliberately causes damage to the property.
- Undertakes repairs without the landlord's consent.
- Causes serious nuisance to the neighbours.

Tenants have many rights in Spain so get to know them.

The Tenant may terminate the rental contract if the landlord:

- Fails to make the necessary repairs to keep the property in a fit and habitable condition.
- Disturbs the tenant's dwelling use.

"How You Can Make Money and Keep Your House Back Home by Renting a Place in Spain"

If you're a UK homeowner (mortgaged or not) then here's a way to live in Spain and generate a regular passive income from your UK property...

Phil, a 55 year-old builder from Warton in Staffordshire, swapped his 2-bed terrace in rainy England for a 3-bed finca in the sunny Murcia countryside and now makes a regular monthly income that requires zero work.

There's nothing unusual in a 55 year old deciding to leave England behind for the warmth of Spain. However, what *does* make this story unusual, is Phil's less-than-perfect beginnings...

You see – although he's been working hard all his life – Phil had no pension or investments to dip into, no long term savings and he had a rather large mortgage with 15 years left to go on his UK home.

So...

No savings

No pension

No investments

No profit from the sale of a home

...doesn't sound like the ideal starting point for a new life in the sun, does it?

Well despite that, Phil now lives in a fantastic home in Spain, which is an ideal base to develop local building contacts for his business there and to continue his search for the ideal place in the sun.

After initially attempting to buy a renovation project in northwest Murcia with a mortgage in Spain, Phil found the Spanish mortgage market wasn't really geared up for an over 50, self-employed, non-national wishing to buy a house that needed a lot of work! In fact, due to his less than ideal situation and many broken promises by his mortgage brokers in Spain (who convinced him none of this would be a problem) the deal on his house fell through roughly 4 months after he'd originally put an offer on the house.

Beaten but not defeated, Phil went back to the drawing board to work out how he could fulfil a lifelong dream of living in Spain.

He concluded that if he could establish a base and an address in Spain, where he could live full time, he'd be able to find work there and search for the house he wanted to buy without having to rush.

Not only that, but he'd have a legitimate address in Spain and could avoid the cost of constant flights and the delays caused by lost post between Spain and the UK. He'd also be in a position to keep on top of the mortgage company for his eventual project.

His plan was simple.

1. Find a building contract to get him started in Murcia
2. Find a place to rent in Murcia while he worked there

Luckily, his daughter had just bought a house that needed a lot of work and so she and her husband employed Phil on a 3-month contract. She also spoke to her neighbours and through local contacts Phil managed to rent a 3-bed finca for less than £180 (€240) a month on a year-by-year basis.

Obviously, with no need for his home in the UK, he decided to rent that out and achieved £550 (roughly €700) per month in income. So, after his UK mortgage payments (of £290 per month) were accounted for this left Phil with roughly £80 left over.

After driving to Spain in his trusty work van he has since found additional building jobs in the area and is almost in a position (with some creative finance raised from his UK home) to put a big deposit on a Spanish home of his own.

Obviously, if you own your home in the UK outright then the potential to generate a large enough income to live off while renting a place in Spain is a viable alternative to buying there. The benefit? You get to try the Spanish lifestyle before you buy!

Phil's Tips:

- Renting in Murcia while renting your home out in the UK is a cheap and easy way to get to know the neighbours and decide if you really want to live here before you commit your money

- If you own a big enough home outright in the UK then you could effectively live in Spain this way forever and benefit from the income your UK home provides (or even cash in and sell it once you know you're not going back)

- If you're planning on getting work out here within the local expat community then believe me it's tougher than you think - you can expect lower pay and tough competition so don't burn your bridges in the UK - it's always good to have an escape plan

PROPERTY OWNER'S GUIDE

Renovating Property in Murcia

PERMISSIONS

In Spain you need building permits for just about anything you do to the fabric of your house. This also includes lots of things that you might be considering doing in the garden. While in the UK you can build a patio, build low decorative and boundary walls, ponds and sheds as well as install or remove partition walls inside without planning permission *technically* all of these things might need a building permit in Murcia.

Much of Murcia's inland area is covered by Natural Parks and protected zones such as official forest areas. If you are fortunate enough to live out in *el campo* think twice before approaching the Ayuntamiento for building permits.

Even if you are out of a protected area, but not in an official urbanised area, you will probably need over 2.5Ha (~ 7 acres) of land to start any major building work. In protected areas this limit rises to 50Ha (over 100 acres!). Two things that you definitely want to avoid are: alerting the Ayuntamiento to something trivial and uncontentious beforehand and the other is forging ahead with major work only to be stopped half way through.

There are two classes of permit that are needed for building work in Spain depending on the scale of the work involved and its potential impact on your neighbours.

Much of Murcia's inland area is covered by Natural Parks and protected zones but even in unprotected areas you may need more than 2.5Ha of land to start any major building work.

The larger works require that you have drawings professionally prepared and submitted along with full project costings including all labour (even if it's your own time!) and materials required. Smaller things (including most of the things that you would be allowed to do in the UK without planning permission) are covered by the term *'obra menor'*.

The decision as to what category of work your job will fall into is ultimately the decision of the Technical Architect at the Ayuntamiento. If you are doing all the work yourself then the Technical Architect will use some rules of thumb as to the costings.

The building licence fee is a percentage of the quotation, and for *'obras menores'* this is often a very small percentage. For these smaller works, once you have the license fee established with the Ayuntamiento's Technical Architect, you will then be given a form to take to another department of the Ayuntamiento. Here you will be given another form to take to the bank and pay a few euros by way of a downpayment on the final fee. Once the bank has taken your money and stamped the form you then take it back to the Ayuntamiento. Within a few months you will get your permit in the post and an invoice for the remainder of the fee.

> *Larger works require that you have drawings professionally prepared.*

ARCHITECTS

For larger projects you will need to submit much more information to the Technical Architect at the Ayuntamiento. You will need architect's drawings and costings (the '*proyecto*'), which must have been stamped by the College of Architects. You will also need a contract with the *Aparejador* (Technical Architect), a copy of the Escritura showing ownership of the land and copies of *NIE* certificates.

The drawings have to be authorised by The College of Architects (the authorising body) who will ensure that it all meets building regulations before being stamped and returned to the architect. He will then hand it all over to you and you must submit it to the Ayuntamiento with an application form. Most people will have to enter into a contract with an *Aparejador* (Technical Architect) who gets paid 30% of the architect's fee for overseeing the build, which is a similar role to the old building inspector in the UK. They should check steelwork, drainage, structure, roof coverings etc.

It can take upto 4 months to receive your licence and you must start work within 12 months and are not allowed to stop work for more than 6 months otherwise the licence becomes invalid.

It can take upto 4 months to get your licence and you must start work within a year.

For the recent renovation of our 3-storey townhouse in Moratalla my husband Marcus and I employed the services of an architect. We were considering replacing the roof but he advised us that to do that we would also need to "lift" the floor below, as new regulations insisted on a 2.5m ceiling height for habitable rooms if major works were carried out. We realised quite quickly that replacing the roof wasn't necessary after all!

With a new build you really do need a licence and if the finished building is not as per drawings and licence details then you may have difficulties getting the certificate of occupation. However, once signed off, most people feel at liberty to, for example, add permanent roofs to terrace beams etc.

If you're not sure whether to apply for a license then it might be best to talk to a few of the neighbours and get their opinions – they should know how things operate – or you could ask at local builder's merchants or a friendly local solicitor/abogado.

It is often best if you can find an architect who is fluent in both Spanish and English. The architect must be able to convey his instructions to the builder and also be able to thoroughly understand your needs.

Your best bet is to find out the name of the architect from someone with a successful project similar to yours. If you cannot find an architect through a current homeowner then visit local real estate agents, bars, phone directories and builders for a list of licensed architects. Licensing is important because the town government will want to see paperwork from the architect ensuring that he or she is skilled.

FINDING & MANAGING BUILDERS

Depending upon the scale of the work involved you can either find yourself a builder through recommendation or get your architect to select builders for you to meet and get quotes from.

There is a strong networking ethos in Spain and they even have a word for it - "Enchufe." This can work in your favour or against you and I've experienced both. When it works in your favour you'll be employing workers who you know, bump into in the bars and streets, whose family you dine with and children you chat to. When it works against you, the recommendation from your estate agent may lead to over priced work and materials, late starts, incorrect permissions and any number of other problems.

In some towns the builders will be so over run with work that they won't even bother returning your call, whilst in other places there's a proliferation of people professing to be builders who are probably more suited to painting and decorating.

The best advice is to get a builder recommended to you. See some of their other work and find out where they live! Get testimonials from happy customers. Get everything in writing from the builder including, where possible, penalties for late starts and finishes.

Get everything in writing from the builder including, where agreed, penalties for late starts and finishes.

Your best solution is to find a builder who is bi-lingual, that way they can understand what you want and also interact with the local ayuntamiento and builder's merchants.

TOOLS AND MATERIALS

If you are looking for the warm feeling that UK DIY superstores offer then you currently need to trek to the north side of Murcia or to Cartagena to visit Leroy Merlin. This out-of-town shop has just about everything but, as with UK DIY retail outfits, expect to pay over-the-odds for your individually shrink-wrapped widgets.

For basic tools and materials you should try your local hardware shop (*ferretería*). From these shops you should be able to get sand, cement, bricks, hand tools, basic plumbing fittings, some paints, floor and wall tiles etc. We would encourage readers to use their local *ferretería* regularly since you'll regret it sorely if they go out of business!

For more 'weird stuff' like fibreglass septic tanks, water pumps for your downstairs deposit, a wider selection of bathroom taps etc., you will be better off going to your nearest large trading estate (*polígono*). The best ones for electrical, building and plumbing supplies we have found are to the west of Murcia in San Ginés, to the northeast of Cartagena and to the west of Lorquí.

You will find that suppliers on these trading estates usually have what you need ex-stock at a good price and they often deliver a decent-sized order for free. Be aware that most of the trade counter outfits only accept cash but this offers a good opportunity for substantial savings compared to the equivalent item ordered locally.

RENOVATION BUDGET

Expensive Items Not Including Furnishings   **ESTIMATED COST**   **ACTUAL COST**

- ☐ Bathroom
- ☐ Doors
- ☐ Flooring
- ☐ Kitchen
- ☐ Landscaping
- ☐ Planning permission
- ☐ Re-wiring of electrics
- ☐ Roof
- ☐ Swimming Pool
- ☐ Terrace
- ☐ Tiling
- ☐ Well
- ☐ Windows
- ☐ Other Structural

Selling Property in Murcia

SELLING YOUR HOUSE

It is strongly recommended that you take legal advice when you decide to sell a property in Spain. Whether you are resident or not there are plenty of pitfalls that a good lawyer should help you avoid.

SELLER'S TAX LIABILITY

The seller is usually responsible for the payment of capital gains tax. The seller should also pay any fees for the cancellation of any loans on the property, for example, the mortgage.

In the recent past the seller has declared a much lower sale price in order to reduce the tax burden. This process, while not as widespread as in the past, is still happening in many parts of the region. Going along with this can get you into trouble as there is a strong chance that the tax office will make an assessment and give the seller or buyer a tax bill and potentially a fine.

TAX DEPOSIT FOR NON-RESIDENT PROPERTY SALES

To avoid the possibility of a non-resident property owner selling their property and running away with all the cash the Spanish government has a requirement that 5% of the declared sales price is witheld by the buyer and deposited with the Spanish Tax Office.

Get legal advice - whether you are resident or not there are many pitfalls a good lawyer will help you avoid.

Once the seller's tax liability (capital gains tax) is assessed they will either be required to pay more or will be given a refund.

Renting Your Property in Murcia

A very popular option when buying a house here is to rent it out to other people. Some buyers decide to do this as a business, others just to rent their property to friends and family. Whatever your choice, there are laws, rules and tips below.

BUY TO LET

If your goal is to buy a property to rent it out then here are some suggestions and thoughts before you get started:

- ❑ What type of rental are you looking for? Potentially more lucrative but less guaranteed holiday lets or long-term rental with lower rates but more security?

- ❑ Be very clear about your purpose. Is it more important that you can get rental income or that you buy a property in a location that you also love?

- ❑ Consider the demographics of the people likely to rent your property in the area you've selected. Will your chosen property appeal to that type of person? Is the size, location and range of facilities etc. acceptable?

- ❑ Use the internet to check comparable properties. How much of the year are they booked, what prices are they charging and what do they offer?

Above all do your homework and take financial advice. Be wary of the promises made by some developers in the region that they will guarantee rental periods and rates – someone will be paying for this – probably you!

- For holiday lettings check the number of flights to your destination. Will this cover your season? Many airlines reduce the number of flights and indeed stop some routes during the winter.

- For long-term rentals consider who you will be marketing to – professionals, families, students etc. Will the local economy provide an adequate supply of tenants?

- Look for a property with something a bit special, a wow factor. This will really help when you are marketing it.

- Crunch the numbers!

Check that you will legally be able to rent out your property and any rules that may apply before you buy it.

RENTAL LAW IN MURCIA

First of all, before you buy, check that you will be legally allowed to rent out your property. Check this with someone other than the person/company you are buying from. Your local Ayuntamiento would be the first port of call in towns and the countryside. If you're buying on an urbanization then you can check with the Community President to understand the rules and if there are any other requirements.

You may need liability insurance to cover damage caused by guests and you should take out buildings and contents insurance for your own peace of mind.

Use a rental contract for all bookings. You can find these on the Internet or go to a *Gestor* and get one drawn up for a small fee.

Legal provisions on renting and letting in Spain are contained in the Law of Urban Lettings (*Ley de Arrendamientos Urbanos*) of 1994, which applies to rental contracts dated from January 1st 1995. According to the law, rental contracts shall be firstly governed by the agreement between the parties (when this exists) and secondly by the Law of Urban Lettings. So it really is necessary to get a contract drawn up to protect yourself.

The landlord is liable to pay income tax at a rate of 25%, assuming that he is a non-resident. You can deduct maintenance expenses from your Spanish income tax.

You must pay tax on rental income in Spain. You must register with the Hacienda your intention to let your property. Do not be tempted to hide your rental income as there has recently been a crackdown and people are being fined anything upto €20,000.

RENTAL TIME PERIODS

Both parties agree the term for which the property will be rented. You may rent the property for a long or a short term. The distinction is very important as Spanish law provides fewer rights to short-term tenants.

Short term rental contracts

Short-term rental contracts (*contrato de arrendamiento de temporada*) require that the tenant vacate the property when the contract ends. This type of contract is normally used for holiday letting. The short-term condition must be specified in the contract and the duration may run for up to 1 year.

Long-term rental contracts

For rentals of durations of more than 1 year you will need a long-term rental contract. If the contract does not exceed 5 years in duration it will be renewed automatically upon its expiration unless the tenant is not willing to renew it. The landlord is obliged to accept these renewals except if previously stated in the contract that he needs to recover the property for his own use before the end of the 5-year period.

After the 5 years are up, the owner may terminate the contract provided that they have given the tenant 30 days notice before the end of the contract; otherwise the contract will be automatically renewed for 3 years unless the tenant refuses this renewal. When there is no duration specified in the rental contract it will run for 1 year.

For longer term rentals of more than 1 year you will need a long-term rental contract.

RENTING YOUR PROPERTY

Make sure your first step is a booking contract stating the full terms and conditions. A standard contract should cover:

- ❏ Arrival and departure times
- ❏ Names of occupants and their contact numbers
- ❏ Payment terms – often a non-refundable booking deposit followed by staged payments
- ❏ Cancellation terms
- ❏ Security deposits – which should be taken before handing over the keys and should cover you for any damage incurred
- ❏ Your expectations of them! Smoking? Pets? Maximum occupancy? Security measures?
- ❏ Responsibility for insurance – their personal possessions will not be covered by your policy!
- ❏ Community regulations – if on a community what must they do about parking, use of the pool etc.?

Ensure funds have cleared before handing over the keys to your property.

Ensure the funds have cleared before handing over the keys.

Give the holidaymakers or long-term renters your contact number (or the number of your local representative) in case of emergency.

Provide your cleaning company with an inventory and checklist and ensure they cover it at every changeover.

Resources

This section needs your help. If you have a business that caters to people wanting to buy property in the Murcia area then get in touch at *www.nativespain.com* - your business details should be in this list!

ESTATE AGENTS

www.kyero.com - covers the whole of Spain
www.dreamspain.net
www.girasolhomes.co.uk
www.direct2spain.co.uk
www.spanish-country-houses-properties.com
http://homes.nativespain.com - listings for renting or buying
www.espana.com - 680 626 213
www.sunsetestates.co.uk - Sunset Estates - UK: 0161 799 9037
www.bestpriceproperties.com - 349 657 201
www.hartlandproperty.com - 968 171 228
www.kingdom-homes.com - 868 944 464
www.simplymurcia.com
www.casacalidaproperties.com - 968 19 33 88
Iberian Properties International - 966 798 068

The North West
ISNOE Gestion Inmobiliaria - Caravaca de la Cruz - 968 722 262
Inmobiliaria Herrero, S.L. - Bullas - 968 654 848
www.infincasa.com - In Fin Casa - Mortalla - 968 730 529

Murcia
Harighi International - Murcia City - 968 904 517

The North East

Inmobiliaria Arabi – Yecla – 968 790 409
Campillo Inmobiliaria – Yecla – 968 750 213
Look and Find – Yecla – 968 753 330
Best House Grupo – Yecla – 968 718 589
Rural Corporations – Jumilla – 968 781 385
Inmobiliaria Rodenas – Jumilla – 968 782 979
Inmobiliaria El Castillo – Jumilla – 968 757 169
Inmotasa – Jumilla – 968 716 264

The South West

Aledo – Alhama de Murcia – 968 630 358
Casas de Lorac – Lorca – UK 0844 734 8057
Inmobilorca – Lorca – 968 477 345
www.inmobiliariapiqueras.com – Totana – 968 423 269
www.m-millenium.com – Totana – 618 103 596
Murcia Select – Lorca – 950 120 904
www.villascostacalida.com – Totana – 968 421 092
Villas Solmar Inmobiliaria – Totana – 968 484366

Águilas & Mazarrón

www.costacalida-estates.com – Isla Plana – 968 152 249
www.bricasa.net – Puerto de Mazarrón – 968 154 537
Aima Inmobiliaria – Mazarrón – 968 592 834
Amici – Puerto de Mazarrón – 968 594 080
www.anotherworldproperties.net – Mazarrón – 968 592 679
www.montemarvacaciones.com – Urb. El Alamillo – 968 153 515
www.pueblosalado.com – Puerto de Mazarrón – 968 594 937
www.bluesky-property.com – Puerto de Mazarrón – 968 154 647
Bolmar Inmobiliaria - Puerto de Mazarrón – 968 153 635
Cafe del Mar – Bolnuevo – 968 156 538
Climasol - Mazarrón – 659 082 619
Construcciones e Inmobiliaria Oromaza – Mazarron – 606 40 20 12
Dolphin Villas – Camposol – 669 512 273
www.euro-casas.com – Puerto de Mazarrón
www.espagna-homes.com – Águilas – 950 466 044

Fujoma - Puerto de Mazarrón - 968 15 40 00
Gest. Inmobiliaria Brisamar - Puerto de Mazarrón - 968 594 262
www.inmobiliariamorales.com - Puerto de Mazarrón - 968 594 749
www.laoficinadeemilio.net - Puerto de Mazarrón - 968 154 186
www.luzdelsol.net - Puerto de Mazarrón - 968 332 011
www.maserworld.es - Puerto de Mazarrón - 968 595 824
www.mazalia.es - Puerto de Mazarrón - 968 332 013
www.mazarronproperties.com - Puerto de Mazarrón - 968 153 813
Promociones Inmobiliarias Parver - Mazarrón - 968 592 776
www.proser2000.com - Puerto de Mazarrón - 968 332 009
www.inmobiliariamazarron.com - Mazarrón - 968 333 047
www.reef3000spain.com - Puerto de Mazarrón - 968 158 425
www.spanishsunset.com - Puerto de Mazarrón
www.sunseaproperties.net - Puerto de Mazarrón - 968 153 325

Cartagena & The Campo de Cartagena
Gestion Inmobiliaria Pv - Fuente Álamo - 968 598 898
www.inmobaltorreal.com - Fuente Álamo - 968 596 103
www.eraspain.com - Cartagena - 968 527 373
Inmobiliaria Doeman - Cartagena - 968 316 200
www.inmonegocios.com- Cartagena - 902 929 252
www.parasolproperties.net - Cartagena - 968 150 088
www.donpiso.com - Donpiso - Cartagena - 968 321 382

Mar Menor
Villa Menor Inmobiliaria - Los Nietos - 968 133 580
Geinsa Inmobiliaria - Los Nietos - 968 133 538
Live Med Coast Sl. - Los Alcázares - 968 144 477
Costa Linda Internacional SL - Los Alcázares - 968 170 728
MiroDali Properties C.B. - Los Alcázares - 968 170 398
Alhambra Villas - Los Alcázares - 968 574 351
Everyday Estates - Los Alcázares - 968 334 556
Swing Land Estates - Los Alcázares - 968 583 209
Alcazares Real Estate - Los Alcázares - 968 574 459
Asset Realty Inmobiliaria, S.L. - Los Alcázares - 968 171 250

SOLICITORS, LAWYERS & NOTARIES

www.iabogado.com – You can get email and telephone consultations for a one-off fixed fee

www.sun-lawyers.com - Solicitor/Notary/Gestor – Calasparra – 968 746 813

www.spainlawyer.com - comprehensive legal information in English. You can also get email and telephone consultations for a one-off fixed fee

www.strongabogados.com

www.daniel-cano.co.uk - English speaking lawyers with offices throughout Spain

www.notariado.org - find a notary and other information on the role of notaries in legal procedures

MORTGAGE & FINANCE

www.blevinsfranksinternational.com - 30 years experience helping expatriates improve and protect their wealth

www.bestmortgage.es - includes a breakdown of the costs involved in buying a property and a glossary of terms used in the buying process

www.casahipoteca.com

www.interest.com - 12 different calculators

www.europamortgages.com - Costa del Sol based mortgage broker offering a wide range of mortgages without arrangement fees

www.spanishmortgagecompany.com

www.tiendahipoteca.es

ACCOUNTANTS

www.spainaccountants.com - English speaking accountants who can process your tax payments online via email and telephone

CURRENCY EXCHANGE

www.currenciesdirect.com

www.escapecurrency.com

www.hifx.com - one of the most well-known forex brokers

www.moneycorp.com

www.travelex.com

www.escapecurrency.com - offer an FX Rate Tracker and foreign currency you can pick up at airports

www.worldwidecurrencies.com - efficient personal service from this company based in London

BANKS

www.activobank.com - ActivoBank

www.bancamarch.es - Banca March

www.batlantico.es - Banco Atlántico S.A.

www.bbva.es - Banco Bilbao Vizcaya (BBVA)

www.bde.es - Banco de España (BDE)

www.bancsabadell.com - Banco de Sabadell

www.bancovitoria.es - Banco de Vitoria S.A.

www.bancoesfinge.es - Banco Esfinge S.A.

www.banesto.es - Banco Español de Crédito S.A. (Banesto)

www.bancoetcheverria.es - Banco Etcheverria

www.bancofar.es - Bancofar S.A.

www.bancogallego.es - Banco Gallego

www.bancogui.es - Banco Guipuzcoano

www.halifax.es - Banco Halifax Hispania S.A.

www.bancoinversion.es - Banco Inversión

www.bancopastor.es - Banco Pastor S.A.

www.bch.es - Banco Santander Central Hispano

www.bancourquijo.es - Banco Urquijo

www.bancozaragozano.es - Banco Zaragozano

www.ebankinter.com - Bankinter S.A.

www.bankpyme.es - Bankpyme

www.barclays.es - Barclays Bank S. A.
www.bbk.es - Bilbao Bizkaia Kutxa (BBK)
www.bsnbanif.es - BSN Banif S. A.
www.citibank.com - Citibank
www.commerzbank.de - Commerzbank
www.deutsche-bank.es - Deutsche Bank
www.fibanc.es - FIBANC Banco de Finanzas e Inversiones S.A.
www.bancopopular.es - Grupo Banco Popular
www.hsbc.es - HSBC Bank plc
www.iberagentes.es - Iberagentes Popular Banca Privada
www.ingdirect.es - ING Direct
www.lloysbank.es - Lloyds TSB Bank plc
www.solbank.com - Solbank
www.uno-e.com - UNO-E Bank S.A.

PROPERTY RENTALS

www.rentalsystems.com - all in one service for buy-to-let owners allowing you to take credit card bookings and sample rental contracts with advertising on www.villarenters.com and much more.

www.escapelet.com - list your rental property for free

www.realdata.com/product/16179.shtml - free software that lets you calculate rates or return, refinancing, loan to value ratio, amortization schedule, loan comparison, break even ratio and more.

www.inspectahomespain.com - provides examples of common snagging problems and snagging inspection services throughout Spain.

www.kyero.com - offers free translation of all the core advertising phrases you will need

www.rentalia.com/owner/legal.cfm - sample rental contracts in 7 different languages

EMPLOYMENT

ec.europa.eu/eures/home.jsp?lang=en - European Job Mobility Portal with job offers in 31 countries and useful information on working in Europe.

Online Job Portals

www.ambientjobs.com
www.empleo.net
www.exposure-eu.com
www.globalrecruiter.com
www.faster.es
www.infoempleo.com
www.infojobs.net
www.jobsabroad.com
www.jobtoasterspain.com
www.laborman.es
www.miltrabajos.com
www.monster.es
www.oficinaempleo.com
www.paginas-amarillas.es
www.recruitspain.com
www.secretariaplus.com
www.talentsearchpeople.com
www.thinkspain.com
www.trabajar.com
www.trabajos.com
www.wemploy.com

Temp Agencies

www.adecco.es
www.empresasiman.com
www.iman.com
www.flexiplan.es
www.manpower.es
www.randstad.es
www.select.es
www.tutor-rrhh.com

GOVERNMENT

www.seg-social.es - Seguridad Social
www.extranjeros.mtas.es - Immigration and Emigration
www.aeat.es - Tax Office
www.dgt.es - Vehicle Licensing
www.mec.es - Ministry of Science and Education
www.mtas.es - Ministry of Work and Social Affairs
www.mir.es - Ministry of the Interior
www.meh.es - Treasury
www.map.es - Ministry for Public Administration
www.dnielectronico.es - Electronic DNI
www.fomento.es - Ministry of Public Works
www.mae.es - Ministry of Foreign Affairs
www.mviv.es - Housing Ministry
www.gksoft.com/govt/en/es.html - Regional Government Bodies

NEWSPAPERS, MAGAZINES & JOURNALS

In The UK

www.livingspain.co.uk - Living Spain - ☎ 00 44 01234 710992
www.aplaceinthesunmag.co.uk - A Place in the Sun - ☎ 00 44 01737 786 800
www.livingabroadmagazine.com - Living Abroad Magazine – ☎ 00 44 0131 226 7766

In Spain

www.murciagazette.com - *North West Murcia Gazette*
www.costablancanews.es – Costa Blanca News
www.thecbfriday.com - The CB Friday
www.thinkspain.com
www.laverdad.es - La Verdad
www.laopiniondemurcia.es - La Opinion
www.reporternewspaper.com - The Reporter - ☎ 618 549283
www.informernews.org - The Informer

RECOMMENDED READING

David Hampshire, Buying A Home in Spain 2006, Survival Books, ISBN 190113069X

David Hampshire, Living and Working in Spain 2006, Survival Books, ISBN 19011307464

Alec and Erna Fry, Finca: Renovating an Old Farmhouse in Spain, Santana Books, ISBN 8489954267

Sally Roy, The AA Map & Guide to Costa Blanca, AA, ISBN 0749543353

Spain, Lonely Planet, ISBN 0864424744

Juan Pablo Avisón, Guía Viva Murcia, Anaya Touring Club, ISBN 8481659983

The Rough Guide to Spain, Rough Guides, ISBN 1843532611

Collins Bird Guide, Collins, ISBN 0007113323

Teresa Farino and Mike Lockwood, Travellers' Nature Guides Spain, Oxford University Press, ISBN 0198504357

Marcus and Debbie Jenkins, Going Native in Murcia (second edition), NativeSpain.com, ISBN 1905430213

Yolanda Solo, Spain: The Expat Survival Guide, NativeSpain.com, ISBN 1905430310

For a bookshop in Spain with a good collection of English language titles, as well as games, visit your local Bookworld España store. www.bookworldespana.com

MORE LINKS

A complete and up-to-date list of web links to estate agents, language learning resources, hotels, travel companies and other useful contacts for visitors and investors in Murcia can be found at *www.nativespain.com*

RELOCATION BUDGET

It is not just the costs you will incur in Spain you have to consider when you move, but also the liabilities you are leaving behind.

At Home...	ESTIMATED COST	ACTUAL COST
Mortgages, utilities, taxes, and maintenance		
Savings, insurance and life assurance plans, payments		
Removals		
In Spain...		
20% -30% deposit for the purchase of a property		
Rental accommodation while looking for a property		
Mortgage payments		
Purchase of a new car (or two) if you are not bringing one with you		
School fees		
Renovation budget		
Furniture and fittings		
A monthly "wage" until you can find work		
Mobile phone bills		
Social security/private health cover costs		
Company set up costs if you plan to start your own business		
Taxes – on property, rental income, cars...		

CHANGE OF ADDRESS CHECKLIST

Type	Name	Date Told		Address Given
Bank			❏	
Savings Accounts			❏	
Doctor			❏	
Electric			❏	
Gas			❏	
ISA			❏	
Pension			❏	
Stocks			❏	
Water			❏	
Child Benefit			❏	
Telephone			❏	
Will			❏	
Accountant			❏	
Credit Cards			❏	
Store Cards			❏	
Council Tax			❏	
Health Insurance			❏	
Stocks & Shares			❏	

About Debbie Jenkins

Debbie Jenkins is an entrepreneur, author, publisher and was a life-long city dweller who always longed for a place in the countryside. Her greatest excitement is in owning trees – hundreds of them!

MY STORY

"Eh, hombres, enhorabuenas!" Miguel El Gordo shouted at me and my husband Marcus, over the din of that night's "entertainment."

The second night of our *fiesta* was punctuated with the clamour of a heavy rock band. It was two in the morning and they had only just begun – over three hours later than advertised. But that wasn't their fault; the electrical generators in the disused quarry just couldn't cope with the "10,000 watts of sound and 24,000 watts of light!" They had already blown two generators the size of small cars and were now on their third!

The quarry was heaving. The *sobrasada* and *cerveza* were flowing. Young children were screaming with glee and racing around the legs of tables, adults and the makeshift beer tents. Even the oldest partygoers were raring to go on all night – dancing, gyrating and generally enjoying the party atmosphere.

"Congratulations for what?" we screamed back in between the chorus and the big guitar solo.

"You're on the fiesta committee for next year!" Miguel grinned and then he winked, coughed, spat and ambled off to tell his good news to our other friends in the village.

So, we'd been accepted. After 18 months living in this totally Spanish village of 101 people, we were now on the inside of the most important part of village life – the *Fiesta Patronale*.

Three years earlier we'd decided to leave the hustle and bustle of the city behind and find a better quality of life where the climate and the people were much warmer.

Buying Property in Murcia

Before we moved we lived in a 3 storey Victorian terraced house in the UK's second largest city - Birmingham. My husband, Marcus, had a well-paid career with an International consulting company and I ran my publishing business from offices in the city centre. Our family was in striking distance, we had plenty of friends and what most would consider a good life. But we yearned for something more.

Though we were active members of our community in Birmingham – we ran the local Neighbourhood Watch and Resident's Association and were governors of a large secondary school – we never really felt that there was much of a community to belong to to begin with.

I suppose what we really wanted was to live somewhere where we felt part of a bigger whole, where people still had time to just stop and chat, where they enjoyed life and made time for each other.

During our travels over the years – and especially our trips to Spain – we found that the level of local community involvement was much higher. The people, as a rule, are more gregarious, they respect the elderly, adore the young and they take enjoying themselves very seriously.

So, we wanted to swap grey concrete, monotony, anonymity, rain, crime and stress for mountains, oceans, trees, variety, a sense of belonging, sunshine, adventure and relaxation. We got La Murta on the Costa Cálida in Southern Spain. Perfect.

It took us almost two years to find our perfect spot after visiting the country 8 times! We knew we wanted to be a part of real Spain so we avoided the expat and tourist hotspots and looked for places well off the beaten track. We were also unsure about property right on the coast, being concerned about its bad reputation for over development and too many Brits. However, we didn't want to let second hand information determine our decision so we "did" the coast in early 2002.

We'd been unimpressed with the Costa del Sol – too touristy. Alpujarras - too cliquey. Almería - too plasticky. Not being at all picky (yeah right!) we ended up on the Costa Cálida in the Murcia region, with low expectations and little information.

The cave house, which we eventually bought, was the first house we wanted to see and the last one the estate agent wanted to show us. They were far more interested in trying to shift pig farms in the barren valley - including several places that weren't on our short list. Eventually, after hours trying to persuade us that we'd "get used to the smell", they showed us the house we actually wanted to see at about 5pm, on a very hot May day.

We knew straight away that we wanted it. We'd seen about 50 houses at that point, all along the coast and all in different states of (dis)repair. There were only two others that we liked. But as soon as we saw this house, we just looked at each other and tried to contain our excitement.

The location was perfect - it's just in the foothills of mountains taller than the tallest mountains in the UK, half an hour from the airport, with a new airport being built close by too (if all goes to plan!) And just over half an hour from the nearest sea, the Mar Menor, Spain's inland lagoon. In fact we had approximately 250 miles of beach to choose from, the furthest drive being 1 hour.

Marcus can speak Spanish, so we returned when we thought the neighbours would be around so we could get the real story. The property is one of 3 small houses, two of which are cave houses, set 1km outside a small village of 99 (101 counting us now) inhabitants.

We chatted to our would-be neighbour, and now close friend, David, a stocky, handsome and hard-working man in his 80's who fled to France when Franco was in power. He showed us the exact boundaries of the land; something the estate agent had been unable to do and as we walked around the land - all 6.5 acres of it - our love affair with it grew even more.

The next day we got all our credit cards, bank cards and what cash we had. Raided all the bank machines and got together the deposit of 20% - approx £4,000 ($8,000).

We made the offer and paid the deposit, signed a few documents and went back to England. That part took about half an hour and two months later the deal was complete.

Here's what we bought for £20,000 ($40,000) - the estate agent's spiel, in full:

```
"Approx 20,000 m² land (permitted to build) part
hillside part flat, planted with almonds, carob and
 olives, also large shed/warehouse with 3 caves at
   rear, mains electricity possible, set in the
 foothills of the Sierra de Carrascoy, nice views,
 2km to small pretty village, 5km to town, access
                    fair/good."
```

As it's a cave house it's not the usual renovation project! We've spoken with a number of builders and architects who all have different ideas of what we should do. In the meantime, we decided to build a second property, which is complete, so we now live in this second house while we manage the cave renovation project.

Owning such a remote place does provide its challenges however. We have to have water delivered by lorry where leaky plumbing between the "water cubes" and our house is an expensive, and all too frequent, inconvenience. We had no toilet facilities (as the building work on our drainage system wasn't quite complete) for 3 weeks after we moved in and our electricity relied on 2 small petrol generators and car batteries for over a year. Thankfully, we've now got mains electricity, which was by no means as simple and easy as the estate agent's description suggested!

Neighbours take on greater importance out in the countryside of Spain too.

In England you can live in a street of 400 people in terraced houses, hear their arguments, love-making, eating and fun – and never really know them. Here, in Spain, you are immediately adopted into the Spanish families, welcomed, fed, educated, entertained and good naturedly interrogated about what you've been up to. In return you provide them with news, stories and an exotic slice of a different world.

When we were researching and writing *Going Native In Murcia* we had the privilege of visiting every town and lots of the villages in the region. We fell in love with the North West part of the area, in particular Moratalla. With its winding roads, narrow bends, tall, tottering houses that almost touch across the street and friendly inhabitants, we were smitten. But we didn't want to leave our home in La Murta. So we did the next best thing, we took my brother and his wife there and they fell in love with it too. They now own a 4-storey, jigsaw-piece shaped house, nestled next to a bakery.

When we were helping them look for houses to buy we realised the potential in the area; it has the most *casas rurales* in the whole of Murcia, the location is stunning, rural tourism is on the increase, we couldn't resist. So we bought a 3-storey town house in the *casco antiguo* too. We've had it renovated by my father, who's a builder and now lives over here as well! We did our figures before buying to be sure that the growth and rental income would all work out great, and so far our plan is working.

Other "chores" include walking our two dogs – Dani and Fuggles – who often run off only to come back tired, smelly but extremely happy hours later. We are in the natural park, so walks up the mountain and around the pine forests and *ramblas* (dried up river beds) are a twice daily event.

Since moving here we've become active and enthusiastic scuba divers and most Sundays we'll be found under the water of the Mediterranean. We're spoilt for choice for dive sites; within an hour we can be at the coast and geared up for a dive.

I cook and prepare fresh food almost every day, usually fresh local salad and locally butchered meat or fish. We live in an area that is known as the "market garden", so we have an abundance of local produce. The "food miles" have reduced enormously – more like "food feet" now. When we do eat out the price for a 3-course lunch (including wine) during the week is less than 10Euros (£7/$14) and it is excellent quality.

I say on a regular basis that the Spanish "take having fun seriously". They live a full life here. They spend time with friends and families. They make an effort to enjoy themselves on a regular basis and fill their lives with fun. By being selected for the fiesta commission we've effectively been accepted into the most sacred aspect of village life. The fact that we're foreigners – *mad ingleses* – to boot is also testament to the inclusiveness and warmth of our new neighbours and validates our reasons for moving here.

NativeSpain™.com

Be in the next guide...

We're committed to ensuring the quality of our guides and as such have set up a free membership site for readers and natives to share their hot tips and updates...

Find out all about Spain's towns, cities, culture, beaches, restaurants and more.

Use the diary feature to share your story, as it unfolds, with other expats and would-be expats in Spain. Learn from other people's successes and mistakes in the forums.

Join FREE and get involved at...

www.NativeSpain.com

We look forward to welcoming you to our growing community!

www.bookshaker.com

NativePortugal.com

Buying Property in
Portugal

Gabrielle Collison

Insider tips on buying, selling and renting | 2007

www.bookshaker.com

A BRIT'S SCRAPBOOK

GOING NATIVE IN MURCIA

SECOND EDITION

The Essential Guide for Visitors, Expats & Homebuyers

MARCUS JENKINS
DEBBIE JENKINS

FREE FLIGHTS TO BE WON

PRAISE FOR 'GOING NATIVE IN MURCIA'

The book is literally packed from cover to cover with the most incredibly well researched and pertinent, up to date and relevant information that anyone - and I mean anyone - interested in buying property in Murcia, living in the region or just travelling around Murcia will ever require.
Every scrap of information that Debbie and Marcus Jenkins have gleaned over the past four years is in this book! I love it! It makes fantastic, interesting and even entertaining reading for anyone with even just a modicum of interest in Spain!
Rhiannon Williamson - www.shelteroffshore.com

As the book is full of very relevant web-site addresses, the content is actually much larger than presented... and will remain fresher... longer!
Expat... would be expat... or just visiting Murcia for a holiday... this book is essential reading... don't go without it!
John Mellor (Cheshire/Estrella de Mar)

We are coming back out to Murcia in April and have found your book to be an excellent starting point for the areas and things we need to be looking at. Both my wife and I both found the book very valuable in getting to know Murcia a little better.
John Wilson

We purchased your book via Amazon before Xmas and have found it a most useful guide to the area. Congratulations again on a brilliant, practical book.
Rosemary Clarke

Thanks to your book I have already started the ball rolling towards our move to Murcia and have had a meeting with an agent's representative who happens to be here in Cowes to spend the holiday with relations.
Ken Meynell

Purchased Going Native in Murcia prior to our first visit to that region in September of this year. The book is well researched and covers a whole range of information and many excellent website addresses. A must for anybody considering visiting or purchasing in the Murcia region.
Paul McGloin